UNDERSTAND ACCOUNTS
in NINETY MINUTES

For a complete list of Management Books 2000 titles,
visit our web-site on www.mb2000.com

Other titles in The Ninety Minute Series are:

25 Management Techniques in 90 Minutes
5S Kaizen in 90 Minutes
Active Learning in 90 Minutes
Become a Meeting Anarchist in 90 Minutes
Budgeting in 90 Minutes
Building a Website Using a CMS in 90 Minutes
Credit Control in 90 Minutes
Damn Clients! in 90 Minutes
Deal With Debt in 90 Minutes
Effective Media Coverage in 90 Minutes
Emotional Intelligence in 90 Minutes
Faster Promotion in 90 Minutes
Find That Job in 90 Minutes
Funny Business in 90 Minutes
Getting More Visitors to Your Website in 90 Minutes
Learn to Use a PC in 90 Minutes
Networking in 90 Minutes
Payroll in 90 Minutes
Perfect CVs in 90 Minutes
Plan a New Website in 90 Minutes
Practical Negotiating in 90 Minutes
Run a Successful Conference in 90 Minutes
Strengths Coaching in 90 Minutes
Supply Chain in 90 Minutes
Telling People in 90 Minutes
Working From Home in 90 Minutes
Working Together in 90 Minutes

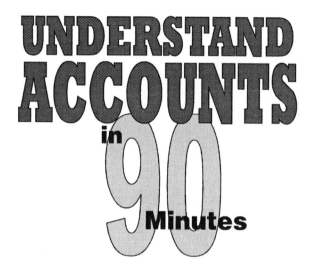

UNDERSTAND ACCOUNTS in 90 Minutes

Chris Turner

2000

First published in 2004 by Management Books 2000 Ltd

Reprinted in 2006 by Managememnt Books 2000 Ltd

Forge House, Limes Road
Kemble, Cirencester
Gloucestershire, GL7 6AD, UK
Tel: 0044 (0) 1285 771441
Fax: 0044 (0) 1285 771055
E-mail: info@mb2000.com
Web: www.mb2000.com

Printed and bound in Great Britain by 4edge Ltd of Hockley, Essex – www.4edge.com

British Library Cataloguing in Publication Data is available
ISBN 1-85252-442-1

Contents

Preface

This book is written for the enormous number of people who are struggling to adapt to the changing world of work and employment in the new millennium.

Throughout the world, new technologies and economic pressures are affecting all sectors of industry, commerce and government. Every type of organisation is having to look at ways to be more efficient and to save money, often just to survive. This is leading to dramatic changes for millions of people in their daily work.

Employers now expect an ever increasing number of their staff to take on financial responsibilities and be held responsible for budgets, cost control and profitability. Nowhere is this more apparent than in the public sector, where doctors, nurses, teachers, police, and local government officers must now also be financial managers.

Understanding these terms and concepts is also vitally important for the self-employed or those thinking of setting up their own business. The survival and success of a business requires sound financial management. To the vast majority who have no background or training in financial or accounting matters this is a new and frightening prospect, but it is an essential requirement of their jobs.

Written by a professionally qualified accountant, this book guides the reader:

- to understand and successfully adapt to the modern workplace
- to appreciate essential basic financial and accounting techniques
- to realise that learning these techniques can be made incredibly simple.

Unlike the approach adopted in traditional textbooks, every financial and accounting concept is introduced to the reader as a simple, logical and necessary step in running a business or organisation. In doing so, it strips away the confusion and academic mystique that can be so intimidating to someone new to the subject. Key aspects of the book are:

- it is a light-hearted story, not a dull textbook
- it can be read by anyone in a short time
- it seeks both to entertain and to educate the reader

As the story unfolds, the reader is painlessly introduced to the following business, financial and accounting concepts:

	Chapter
Account	19
Accounting Standards	23
Annual General Meeting	18
Articles Of Association	18
Audit	23
Balance Sheet	20
Book-Keeping	19
Bottom Line	12
Budget	8
Budget Centre	14
Budget Holder	14
Budget Statement	14
Budgetary Control	14
Business Planning	7
Cash Flow Forecast	15
Company Incorporation	18
Companies Acts	23
Companies House	18
Cost Centre	14
Cost Of Goods Sold	12
Cost-Plus Pricing	8
Credit	19
Creditors	21
Debentures	16
Debit	19
Debtors	21
Debtors' Ledger	21

Each concept is further explained in notes at the end of the appropriate chapter.

1

Work Is Getting Harder!

Tom looked round the freshly painted room before concentrating his gaze on the rows of people sitting at the desks in front of him. Some were dressed in jeans and tee-shirts, others in more formal business suits. The youngest looked as if she couldn't have left school yet, whilst the oldest must be beyond retirement age. In between were men and women of all ages.

Having taught many similar classes, Tom was looking forward to what lay ahead with this new class. How long would it take to show them how easy learning could be? Would there be the usual initial fear and resistance to learning new skills? What would trigger the interest of this particular group?

Tom stood up to address them.

'Ladies and gentlemen, welcome to 'Financial Management', but be warned, this is not going to be a conventional teaching course.'

They stared back at him with curiosity.

'Right now, financial management, accounting and many aspects of commerce and business are strange and unfamiliar to you. As far as you are concerned, they are the language and practices of a foreign land.

'My task is to act as your guide and translator as we journey together into this foreign land. After a while you will find that it is not such a strange and confusing place. It's just a question of being guided where to go and then learning the language.

'Consequently, I am not going to spend much time teaching you about financial management. I don't need to, because you already know a lot about it. You probably don't believe me at the moment, but by the time this course has finished you will realise that most financial and accounting principles are based on common sense and logic that is familiar to all of us.

'What we need to do is to look at that logic and understand the language. And by the way, how we go about doing that will be decided by you, not me.'

Tom paused for a moment to let his words sink in, and carefully studied the rows of faces staring back at him.

People were looking at him with surprise. This wasn't what they had expected on a course in financial management. This short, red faced man staring at them through gold rimmed glasses had won their total attention.

'But before we go any further, please would you introduce yourselves and explain why you are here' said Tom.

One by one members of the group stood up and spoke.

'I'm a ward sister at the County Hospital. I am a professionally qualified nurse, but nowadays I am also expected to be a budget holder and be held responsible for the costs of running my ward.'

'I've spent all of my working life in local government, but now we are being broken up into separate divisions and are having to compete with outside private firms who are tendering to do our work. My job will only survive if I know how to run the division as a separate and competitive business.'

'I work for an international computing company. Our head office is being closed down and we are being restructured into smaller regional business units. I am responsible for restructuring our operations in this area. I'm a computer salesman by training, and frankly I don't feel comfortable with what is expected of me.'

'I'm a local builder. I set up in business five years ago on my own, and I now employ eight people. Nowadays I find that I spend all of my time with paperwork and worrying about the bank overdraft rather than working on site.'

'I'm an apprentice hairdresser at a local salon and I shall finish my apprenticeship in three months. I know that the salon won't be taking me on as permanent staff so I want to think about setting up my own business.'

'I retired from the Army last year. I'm 45 years old and I left the Army with a lump sum payment for long service. I want to buy a small business that I can run with my wife, but it worries me that I don't know much about the world of commercial business.'

'I'm a Police Officer, or at least I think I still am! I joined up to catch criminals, but nowadays I spend a lot of time trying to understand the new thinking in resources management.'

One by one, the rest of the class introduced themselves describing their jobs and work experiences.

2

Finance – the Need to Learn

'You obviously come from a wide variety of backgrounds,' said Tom, 'local government, the National Health Service, the Armed Forces, multinational companies, small companies, self-employment, college. And you have all chosen to attend this Financial Management course.

'Why did you do this?

'Because you are interested in finance?

'Because you think the title sounds really exciting?

'Because you think that it will make you rich?

'No, I don't think it was any of those reasons.

'You did it because you are worried. Worried about what is happening in your place of work.

'The old order is changing. You are having to face new responsibilities, areas that you have not been trained in, and that worries you.

'You are being asked to become *accountable*, *financially responsible*, be *budget holders*, take charge of *profit centres* and *cost centres*. In many cases you don't really understand what these words and expressions mean, let alone how they affect you and your job.

'And that worries you, doesn't it? Because you're not sure that you can handle it, and you're scared of what may happen if you can't cope.

'We live in tough times in the modern world of work. There is no such thing as a job for life any longer, and if you can't cope you can't expect to stay in your job.

'And it's the prospect of losing your job that's the really frightening thing.'

Tom paused to let his words sink in. All eyes in the room were fixed on him. He knew that his words were hitting home with most people. They could identify with what he was saying.

'Let's think about why this has come about,' he continued.

'When you first started work you were probably advised by your parents or teachers that you should learn a skill, trade, or profession that would equip you for the world of work and employment. You were told that if you joined a respected company or organisation, you could look forward to the prospect of a safe job for life. Isn't that so?

'So what are you all doing here today?

'What has happened to your safe jobs for life?'

Tom looked round the room, but no-one challenged what he was saying.

'Let's think about some of the changes of recent years.

'The latter part of the 20th Century witnessed tremendous growth in the use of computers in every aspect of work, the so called 'Information Technology'.

'In the 1970s, we saw large scale introduction of computers, but for those of us old enough to remember, these were simply something rather clever used by technical people in another department where we worked. You and I didn't have to know anything about them, and probably our only regular contact with them was receiving a computer generated payslip and bank statements. Actually working with them was left to the bearded characters with flared trousers and corduroy jackets who had the highly esteemed and highly paid title of 'computer programmer'.'

A ripple of laughter followed this colourful characterisation.

'In the 1980s, I recall that things began to change. Beards went out of fashion, flared trousers and corduroy jackets became no-go areas and the traditional computer programmer became an almost extinct creature. But it wasn't just fashion that brought about changes.

'At the end of that decade, along came the harmless sounding 'PC', or personal computer. It slipped in quietly at first. Perhaps a single machine sitting on a desk in a corner of the office. The chances were that only one or two people knew how to use it, and they would jealously guard their new found status. Although they lacked the heavyweight authority and fashion sense of the earlier computer programmers, they enjoyed a sense of importance based on a smattering of computer buzzwords that set them apart from the rest of us.

'Then, in the late 1990s, there was an explosion in the use of PCs. Yes, the wretched things spread all over the place! At work, they popped up on office desks, they crept into schools to grab our children's attention and then infiltrated our homes putting the whole family at risk. No one and nowhere was safe from them!'

This prompted more laughter around the room, and some nodding of heads in recognition and agreement.

'Now, I'm not here to talk to you about PCs or to explain how they work. What I want you to realise is how they are affecting the workplace and your jobs.

'We all know that the old style factories that used to employ thousands of people have gone. Consider the car industry for example. Until the 1970s, hundreds of skilled people worked on assembly lines. Then the Japanese showed us that cars could be built more cheaply and to higher standards using computer controlled robots. By the 1980s, car manufacturers world-wide had to adopt similar technology to compete and survive. This meant that thousands of traditional jobs in the industry were lost for ever.

'Nowadays, it's the PCs that are bringing about the biggest changes. They continue to spread throughout organisations and are having a dramatic effect. Can you give me a few examples?'

Several hands went up in response.

'Everyone in my office now has a PC with a word processing package and so our company doesn't employ as many secretaries. The old typing pool is a thing of the past.'

'We use spreadsheet packages for all sorts of clerical and analytical tasks that used to be someone else's responsibility.'

'Our databases give us individual access to vast amounts of information in seconds that would have taken weeks of work to collate just a few years ago.'

'Email has transformed all communication both inside our company and with our customers and suppliers.'

'The internet is brilliant. I use it for research every day and I can find answers to what I want in a matter of minutes.'

Tom raised his hand to interrupt.

'Thank you, these are all excellent individual examples of what is going on, but let's look a little deeper behind it all.

'What is really happening is that the old clearly defined job structures in the workplace are breaking down. PCs are putting information and power into the hands and control of the individual. This is leading to significant changes in organisational structures. To a very large extent, the old idea of distinctly separate managers and workers has gone. Nowadays the emphasis is on empowering the individual worker to take on management responsibilities.

'But that's only half of the story.

'At the same time every type of organisation is facing tight financial pressures. Competition in industry and commerce increases on a global scale every year, and throughout the world, governments are under pressure to reduce spending. Measuring and controlling the finances has become a top priority for economic survival.

'For many years, most organisations operated with only limited amounts of financial information, typically produced for the entire organisation at the end of each year. But now that we have PCs, it possible to produce much more detailed financial information for individual areas and activities within the organisation which show how well, or badly, each one is performing.

'You don't have to be a financial genius to realise that if the entire organisation is under pressure to perform better, it follows that the people involved in each of those areas and activities will be expected to make sure that they are not wasting or losing money.

'This is occurring all over the world. Whatever an organisation's reason for existence, whether it is to make profits, provide a service, or even act as a charity, it has the need and now the computer technology to look at everything it does in financial terms.

'And as part of the process of putting wide-ranging information and power into the hands of individuals in the organisation, financial information and financial responsibility is being passed down from senior management to individual employees.

'The technology allows the information to be produced, and the individual is expected to be responsible for acting upon it. That's why, as I said earlier, you are being asked to become *accountable* and *financially responsible*.

'Similarly, for those of you who are self-employed, running small businesses or thinking of setting up a new business, there is great pressure on you to understand basic accounting and finance.

'Apart from the crucial aspects of running the business profitably, you are expected to produce and understand detailed financial information for various organisations such as the bank for borrowing money, the Inland Revenue for paying tax, Customs and Excise for paying Value Added Tax, and possibly suppliers and customers who want to be sure that they are dealing with a financially sound business.

'So, no matter what your background or training, nowadays you are expected to understand and contribute to the financial success of your place of work.

'The fact that you have not been trained in financial and accounting matters is not going to stop these developments affecting your workplace. The pressure is on you to make the effort to learn about them if you want to get or keep a job, or to run your own business.

'And we are here to help you to do that.'

3

The Traditional Way to Learn

'Now that you know why accounting and financial management is so important in the modern world of work, it's time to look at it in detail. I'll introduce you to the subject as it was introduced to me many years ago.'

Tom went up to the writing board and began to write.

'Let's start with a look at a **Profit and Loss Account**. Who can help me by saying what this should look like?'

Nobody said anything. Some shuffled nervously, others just looked blank. This did not deter Tom.

'OK, I suggest that you all now listen very carefully and copy down what I am about to put on the board.'

He picked up a felt pen and wrote down lots of words and figures. He wrote quickly and spoke rapidly about each new word or number as he wrote it down. As he wrote the students tried to keep up with him, struggling to see what he was writing with his back to the class.

'OK, has everybody got that?'

Nobody said a word. They just stared blankly at him.

'Excellent, that is a good start', he beamed. 'Now let's introduce you to the **Balance Sheet**.'

Again, he wrote quickly compiling a series of numbers and unfamiliar words on the board. He spoke rapidly as he wrote, hardly bothering to turn to face the class as he did so. Nobody looked at him as he spoke. Everyone was too busy trying to copy down the strange words and numbers.

After he had finished writing he sat down and waited for everyone to finish copying from the board. As the last person finished, he examined the sea of faces in front of him. He noted that they all looked tired, bored and frustrated.

'Right', he said, 'that's enough for today I think. Before we next meet I would like you all to get hold of a suitable textbook, either by buying one at a local bookshop or by borrowing one from a library.'

'I won't recommend any particular titles as there are so many accounting and finance books available nowadays. I'm sure that you won't have any problem in finding something suitable that you will find interesting.'

As the students walked out of the room, he noted with some satisfaction the resentful expressions on their faces.

'Good. It's working,' he thought to himself. 'The usual response. They are already looking bored and fed up.'

4

Traditional Teaching Rejected

At the start of the next session Tom noticed that nearly all of the students had a textbook on their desks. He glanced at the titles:

'*Basic Accounting*'
'*Modern Financial Management*'
'*Finance For Business*'
'*Finance Made Simple*'
'*Introduction To Accounting*'

He picked one up and smiled as he looked at the list of chapters enticing the reader to explore such topics as *Business Planning*, *Budgetary Control*, *Double Entry Book-Keeping*, and *Cash Flow*.

'Well, how have you all got on with your textbooks?' he asked. 'Have you made much progress with them yet?'

No-one said anything. He sensed the hostility towards him. He looked around the room and then settled his gaze on Gill, the ward sister from the County Hospital.

'How have you got on?' he asked her.

'Frankly, not very well', she replied.

'And why is that?' snapped Tom, adopting an unexpectedly aggressive tone to his voice.

Taken aback by his sudden sharpness, Gill replied defensively, 'I'm sorry but I just don't understand it. I tried reading the first two chapters of a book from the library but it doesn't make any sense to me. It's just a load of old jargon and nonsense if you ask me. Lots of complicated words, fancy mathematics and no explanations.'

The rest of the class were now staring at Tom and there were murmurs of approval and agreement with what Gill had said. He could sense their resentment.

Pausing for a moment he replied, 'Yes, you are probably right. Your textbook is full of what looks like jargon and nonsense, but that is only because you don't understand it yet.'

'How can I understand it?' Gill replied sharply. 'Isn't that the purpose of the book, to teach me so that I do understand it?'

'Yes, but ...' Tom tried to intervene, but Gill was now really getting worked up and angry.

'Isn't that exactly why I came on this course so that I can understand it?' she continued.

'I'm fed up, really fed up. Fed up with textbooks and fed up with this course.'

She looked accusingly at Tom.

'Look, I'm a nurse, a trained nurse, and I accept what you said earlier about why we need to understand finance in our jobs, but do you really think you can teach me to be a financial manager in a few lessons?'

She paused to pick up her coffee. She took a sip and turned up her nose in disgust.

'I think that we are all just wasting our time with textbooks, and I have got better things to do than to sit here listening to you and drinking this disgusting coffee.'

'Excellent, excellent,' beamed Tom, 'now we are really getting somewhere'.

5

The Easy Way to Learn

'Ladies and gentlemen, I do believe that we now have the basis for this course,' said Tom.

Turning to face Gill, he asked, 'So, you don't like the coffee. What are you going to do about it?'

'The coffee?' asked Gill in surprise.

'Yes, the coffee. You just said that it is disgusting and you won't put up with it. So what are you going to do about it?'

Gill looked embarrassed. 'Do about it? What do you mean?'

'Could you do any better?' Tom replied.

'I can certainly make a better cup of coffee than this, and for less than the 30 pence I paid for it in the machine.'

'OK, why don't you then?'

'What are you saying? Are you suggesting that I should bring my own flask of coffee to classes?'

Tom smiled. At least he had broken the hostile reaction of the last few minutes.

'You could do,' he replied, 'but has it occurred to you that you may not be the only person in this room who thinks that the coffee is poor quality and expensive?'

Gill paused for a moment before replying. 'Well, I suppose not. But I still don't see what you are getting at.'

'Simple', replied Tom triumphantly. 'I'm suggesting that you do something about the coffee, not only for yourself but for the whole class.'

'Why should I do that?' she responded.

'For three very good reasons –

'Firstly, we can all enjoy a better cup of coffee.

'Secondly, you can probably make some money at the same time.

'Thirdly, and most important of all, in doing so you will learn and understand what business, finance and accounting is all about.'

6

We Can All Run a Business

The people in the room looked intrigued. This certainly was a different approach from the normal style of teaching.

'Are you suggesting that I should organise our own coffee making facilities?' asked Gill.

'Exactly,' responded Tom.

'I'm willing to have a go but I don't know who else is interested.'

'OK, why don't you ask them.'

Gill looked round the room. There were twenty people including herself.

'Is anyone interested in better quality, less expensive coffee?' she asked.

Eleven people held up their hands. That meant that twelve of the twenty people in the room, including Gill, disliked the existing machine coffee.

'What about the rest of you?' she asked. Three people said that they were happy with the machine coffee, and the other five said that they didn't drink coffee.

She looked at Tom. 'It does look like I'm not the only one, so I guess that it is worth trying to do something about it'.

'Congratulations!' beamed Tom. 'Now we are really getting somewhere. That's several business lessons covered in one go.'

'What?' she said in surprise. 'What do you mean?'

Tom smiled again. 'I mean that you have identified a business opportunity for an entrepreneur. Market research indicates that 75% of the population are consumers. 80% of those consumers are dissatisfied with existing sources of supply on grounds of quality and price and represent potential customers.'

'But I never did all that,' said Gill.

'Oh yes, you did,' replied Tom. 'It's just that I've put it into the language of textbooks. As you said earlier, lots of complicated words, fancy mathematics and no explanations.'

'You see,' Tom continued, 'a few minutes ago we found out that you don't like the coffee purchased from the machine. It's poor quality and expensive.

'You then asked the rest of the people here what they thought of the coffee. In a class of 20 people, 15 are coffee drinkers. In business jargon, we call that a population size, and some simple mathematics says that 75% drink, or consume, coffee.

'Of those 15 coffee drinkers, 12 don't think that they are getting good quality or value for money. In other words, and some more simple mathematics, 80% of the coffee drinkers would probably be interested in buying their cups of coffee elsewhere. All that it takes is for someone to organise an alternative supply of cups of coffee. A person who does this is known as an entrepreneur in business language.'

Gill still looked at Tom with some suspicion. 'You've made that sound so simple,' she said, 'but surely that's not going to help us to learn everything we need to know.'

'No,' agreed Tom, 'not absolutely everything, but we shall cover the fundamentals and provide a solid basis to work from. Then, if you feel you need to, you can turn to the complicated textbooks for specific points.

'The key point, however, is that you will realise that you have it in you to grasp these important fundamentals. Running a home, planning a holiday, cooking a meal are all forms of business activity that we are familiar with, and we don't need to consult textbooks to understand them.'

Glancing round the room at the rest of the people, Tom continued.

'What I want you all to realise is that business, finance and accounting stem from very simple and obvious ways of doing things. Despite what you may think, there is no special art, science or magic involved.

'On every course I run in this college I meet people from all walks of life, and in all types of job or business. The modern world is forcing them to understand the basics of finance and accounting. They all start with your dislike of the subject and dull textbooks. They want to get on with their work in those areas that they are familiar with.

'The conventional 'chalk and talk' or textbook approach is of little interest to them, so on each course we explore and reject that approach. In the process we always come up with a different way to understand and learn. As I said to you on the first day, how we go about it is decided by you, not by me.'

Turning to Gill, he continued, 'On this course it looks as if the coffee is going to be our way to tackle the subject. So, I want you to come up with some ideas of how we can do this.'

Concepts

ENTREPRENEUR

A person who sets up a business, and who is prepared to take risks based on initiative and judgement, with the intention of making profits.

MARKET RESEARCH

Activities undertaken to find out where demand for a particular product or service exists, when it exists, and at what price. The principal objective is to establish what quantities should be produced or provided. Information is gathered from various sources including questionnaires, surveys, trade journals, internal and public records. All facts likely to be useful are collected and analysed using mathematical and statistical techniques. Market research is a vital first step in setting up a new business or supplying new products or services.

7

The First Lesson In Business

At the start of the next meeting Tom looked over to Gill. 'How are you getting on with the coffee business?'

'I've given it some thought,' she replied, 'but there is so much to consider that I end up terribly confused.'

'That's a common problem,' replied Tom, 'but don't let it worry you. Let's make it easier for you.'

He walked over to the window and looked out. After a few moments he turned round and explained, 'Think of what you are doing as a journey. You are currently at Point A and you want to get to Point B. So what does that involve?

'First of all, you must have a reason for wanting to be at Point B, an objective or a goal. Why else would you make the journey?

'Secondly, you need to know what direction to take to get to Point B. This requires a plan or a map.'

Tom paused and looked at Gill.

'Are you saying that I need objectives and plans?' she responded.

'That's exactly what I'm saying,' Tom nodded approvingly, 'and what are they?'

Gill thought for a moment. 'I suppose that the objectives are what we said about making better coffee at a cheaper price and to make some extra cash at the same time.'

'Now we really are getting somewhere,' Tom interrupted. 'I shall be happier if I can now introduce you to the concept of the 'profit motive'. That's the expression we use in business for saying that you fancy the idea of making some extra money.'

Tom paused for a moment to let his comments sink in. He then continued, 'And what about your plan?'

'I suppose that's where I don't really know where to begin,' Gill admitted.

'Don't worry,' Tom responded quickly. He laughed and said, 'Most people don't think they understand this sort of thing. Profit motives? Plans? It may sound complicated but it is really all so simple. In fact, it is a part of everyday life for us all.'

Several members of the class looked puzzled.

'Suppose,' said Tom, turning to face Mike the policeman, 'I said to you that I would pay £1 for the newspaper lying on top of your briefcase. What would you do?'

He pulled a £1 coin out of his pocket as Mike replied, 'I'd be happy to sell it to you.'

Tom leaned forward, gave the coin to Mike, and picked up the newspaper.

'Thank you, I'll read this later. Now, please tell everyone why you have sold this to me.'

'Simple,' responded Mike. 'I paid 40 pence for the paper, you offered me £1, so I made 60 pence profit.'

'Excellent,' answered Tom. 'That was a neat demonstration of what is probably the most important and most basic calculation in business and accountancy.

'What we can sell something for, less what we paid for it, gives us an increase in wealth. We all enjoy extra wealth and that's why we go ahead with the deal. Notice, though, that before we go ahead, we check that it's worth doing with a quick sum.'

Tom paused for a moment and then raised his voice to emphasise his words.

'In business jargon, what we have just seen is a Profit Forecast. Profit is defined as Income less Costs. The Profit Forecast is simply a plan or estimate of how much profit we think an activity or business can make over a period of time. It shows us whether it is sensible to go ahead with the business or not. If the profit looks good, we do it. If the profit is too low, or worse still there is a loss, we don't do it.'

Tom paused to let his words sink in.

'As you develop your careers or businesses you will see this fundamental point time and time again.

'You will see it if you are planning a new business or expanding an existing business. Before anyone will lend you money for your business, particularly the bank manager, they will want to see a Profit Forecast.

'As businesses get complicated, so do the Profit Forecasts, and that is when you need the expert help of a professional accountant. But, never lose sight of one thing. The Profit Forecast is simply an estimate of expected Income less expected Costs. It's the basic decision maker for whether to go ahead with the business or not.'

Concepts

BUSINESS PLANNING

The identification of objectives for an organisation and the process of determining the most appropriate policies, strategies and tactics to achieve them. Much of the jargon used in business planning comes from the language of the military and in large organisations is a formal, complicated and extensively documented process. In small organisations it is often not documented but based on an individual's 'gut feelings' and knowledge of the business and market.

PROFIT

Profit is calculated as the excess of income over expenditure, or 'what is left over after all of the bills have been paid'. Concern with making profit (the 'profit motive') is a key driving force for all businesses. Profit is necessary to expand the business, invest in new technology and equipment, and to pay higher wages or shorten the working week.

A business can survive without making profit but will be very restricted in what it can do. Some organisations are specifically set up to be non-profit making, but these are usually owned or controlled by parent organisations, such as national government, which can fund their operations and guarantee their financial security.

The opposite of profit is loss, and no business or organisation can survive excessive losses as it will simply run out of money and be unable to pay its bills and the wages owing to its employees.

PROFIT FORECAST

The principal document produced by the business planning process. It is a detailed statement of the expected income of the organisation, less the expected expenditure, leading to the expected profit. It is a key document for managers and for anyone thinking of investing money in a business. It is an essential requirement for a business or organisation seeking to borrow money from a bank.

8

Plans, Budgets and Sales

At the start of the next meeting Tom looked over to Gill. 'How are you getting on with the Profit Forecast for the coffee business?'

'I've given it some thought,' she replied, 'but to tell the truth, I don't really know where or how to start it.'

'OK,' replied Tom, 'I can see that you are falling into a common trap. You are confused and you are making it more difficult than it really is.'

Turning to address the rest of the class, he said, 'Please would you all tear off a piece of paper and have a pen ready.'

When everyone had done this, he continued, 'You all have one minute to draw a picture of a forest.'

Despite a few puzzled faces everyone in the room began drawing at a rapid pace. Tom walked round the room and looked at their efforts. After sixty seconds he raised his hand and told them to stop.

Addressing Dave, the young man from local government, Tom asked, 'Please tell the class how you went about drawing the forest.'

Dave looked embarrassed, but replied, 'Well, I drew a tree, then another tree, then another tree, and another, until I had what resembles a forest.'

'Thank you,' replied Tom. 'Did anybody do anything different?'

Nobody spoke.

'Good. It is clear that you all did the same thing. Based on a mixture of instinct and common sense you all knew that the only way to draw the forest was to draw in all of the trees, one by one. In other words you tackled the problem by considering its component parts, one by one.'

Tom watched the reaction of the class before continuing. 'Now let's get back to our coffee business Profit Forecast. What can you tell me about it?'

'I suppose that what we should do is to regard it as a series of component parts,' replied Dave.

'Excellent,' beamed Tom, 'And can you suggest where we might start?'

'How about with the Sales?'

'Now we really are getting somewhere,' said Tom. 'How do you think we should go about this?'

'How about making an estimate of how many cups of coffee we are likely to sell?'

'Very good,' said Tom, 'you are developing the idea of a Sales Plan, but there is one more factor we must add. That is the period of time, or planning period, we are going to consider. In business, the most common period of time for planning purposes is one year. I see no reason why we shouldn't also use the period of one year for our coffee business.'

'But when I worked out the profit I would make on the newspaper I sold you I didn't think about any period of time,' interrupted Mike.

'That's not true,' replied Tom, 'you did consider a time period. Your time period was the length of time it took to sell the newspaper. The point is, though, you were only looking at the sale on that one deal. Now, what would you have to think about if you were going to sell your newspaper to me on a regular basis?'

'I see what you are getting at. I would have to calculate how often I would sell you a newspaper. How many times in a week, how many times in a year, and so on.'

'Yes, you've got the idea.' Turning back to face Dave, Tom asked, 'So what about the Sales Plan for the coffee business?'

'Well, there are 12 of us who don't like the existing machine coffee. We have a morning and an afternoon coffee-break, so that's 2 cups each per day. There are 5 college days in a week, and we attend college for 40 weeks in the year.'

Tom stepped forward and handed him a pen. 'Write it up on the board please.'

Dave stood up and wrote the following:

SALES PLAN

Daily Sales   =   **12 Students x 2 cups each** =   **24 cups**

Weekly Sales   =   **Daily Sales x 5 days**   =   **120 cups**

Yearly Sales   =   **Weekly Sales x 40 weeks**   =   **4,800 cups**

He stopped writing and looked at Tom.

'Is that it?' asked Tom.

'I think so,' Dave replied. 'Should there be anything else?'

'That is a perfectly good Sales Plan but it is really only half of what we need,' replied Tom. 'What you are showing is the quantities involved, but if we are going to calculate profit we have to think in terms of money as well. In other words, what is the value of the Sales Plan in £'s. To get that, we need to put in the price of the cups of coffee sold.'

'But we haven't decided on a price yet,' interrupted Dave. 'How do we know at what price to sell?'

Tom was pleased with the progress they were making and replied, 'We've now stumbled into an area called 'Pricing Policy'. It's a simple enough problem, how much should we charge for what we are selling, but it is a crucial factor for business. In broad terms we should charge the price that gives us the most profit, but this can be very difficult to calculate.

'Let's put it another way. If we charge too much for our goods or services, then no-one will buy from us and we won't get any sales income. If we charge too little, we risk selling too cheaply and losing profit or even making a loss. Trying to decide the correct price is a key decision for all businesses, no matter how large or small they are or what industry they operate in.

'In small companies, setting prices is usually left to individual managers who use their judgement and experience of the market and what their customers are willing to pay. In very large companies it is not uncommon to have whole departments working on pricing policy by undertaking market research and using complicated computer based financial models to look at the likely outcomes of charging different prices for the goods and services they sell.'

'That's all very well, but I still don't know what price we should sell the coffee at,' said Dave.

'How about 20 pence per cup,' suggested a voice from the back of the class. 'That's a fair price and it's cheaper than the machine coffee.'

Tom looked at Dave. 'Well?'

'20 pence sounds sensible to me.'

'OK, go back to your Sales Plan and put it in. At the same time, change the word 'Plan' to 'Budget'. When we express a Plan in money terms we call it a Budget.'

Dave went back to the board and changed it to read:

SALES BUDGET

Daily Sales = 12 students x 2 cups each x 20p = £ 4.80

Weekly Sales = Daily Sales x 5 days = £ 24.00

Yearly Sales = Weekly Sales x 40 weeks = £ 960.00

'Good Heavens!' he exclaimed. 'That looks like a lot of money just for cups of coffee!'

'Yes, and it shows you why it is so necessary to prepare budgets,' Tom replied. 'It also helps to make you all realise why the companies and organisations you work for are so concerned every year with the business of budgeting for the year ahead.'

Concepts

PLANS

Business planning leads to individual plans for different areas and departments of an organisation. Plans are normally expressed in terms of expected quantities. For example, a manufacturing company will prepare a 'Sales Plan' for the number of units it expects to sell, a 'Production Plan' for how many units it will produce, a 'Purchasing Plan' for how many units it needs to buy in, and so on.

PLANNING PERIOD, FINANCIAL YEAR

The period of time for which a business plan is prepared and used. It can vary depending upon the nature of the industry, product or service. For example, a holiday tour company may plan for summer and winter seasons of a few months duration, whilst a civil engineering company or government department may plan to build a motorway that will take several years to complete.

The most common planning period in business is for a period of 12 months and is referred to as the 'Financial Year'. (This should not be confused with the government's Financial or Fiscal Years which relate to the periods used for assessing taxes).

PRICING POLICY

The policy used by a business to set the prices of its goods or services. A common method is 'cost-based' or 'cost-plus' pricing where a standard percentage mark-up is added to the cost of producing the goods or service. This is used by many shops where a percentage mark-up is added to the cost at which they buy goods for resale.

In other instances, the policy is to set the price in response to the prices charged by competitors, or in response to what customers are prepared to pay. Industries such as airlines have extremely complicated pricing policies which have to be competitive but also cover a wide range of services ranging from 'economy' to 'first-class'.

BUDGET

A plan expressed in financial terms for a specific future period (e.g. 'Sales Budget' expressing the financial value of planned sales). Large, medium-sized and most small companies prepare written budgets for the year ahead, normally using computer spreadsheets. At Government level the Chancellor prepares 'The Budget' for determining public spending and setting taxes. At a personal level budgets may be prepared by individuals or households based on personal income and spending plans.

9

Direct Costs

At the end of the previous session, Tom had asked everyone to think about the costs involved in setting up the coffee business for the class. Turning to Gill, he asked, 'What progress have you made?'

Gill opened her notebook before replying, 'I've been finding out what we would need. If we are going to improve the quality of the coffee I suggest that we look at filter coffee machines. I've got some details of what it would cost to buy a large enough machine and the cost of ingredients.'

'Excellent,' interrupted Tom. 'This looks like the start of a Business Plan. Please write on the board the costs that you have in your notebook.'

Gill wrote down the following costs :

COST OF INGREDIENTS

Coffee	£ 2.50 per box
Filters	£ 2.00 per box
Milk	£ 0.36 per pint
Sugar	£ 0.80 per bag

'Thank you,' said Tom. 'So how much will it cost to make a cup of coffee?'

'I don't really know,' she replied.

'That's because we need more information,' said Tom.

'What you need to do is to calculate how many cups each of those individual ingredients will make. Please have a go at estimating this, and then you can work out the total cost of ingredients per cup of coffee.'

Gill picked up the pen again and wrote the following:

COST OF INGREDIENTS

Coffee: £ 2.50 per box - makes 50 cups = £ 0.05 per cup

Filters: £ 2.00 per box - makes 50 cups = £ 0.04 per cup

Milk: £ 0.36 per pint - makes 12 cups = £ 0.03 per cup

Sugar: £ 0.80 per bag - makes 40 cups = £ 0.02 per cup

Total Cost Of Ingredients = £ 0.14 per cup

'What you have there,' Tom explained, 'is the Direct Cost of making a cup of coffee. It's also sometimes called the Variable Cost. That wasn't too painful was it?'

'No,' Gill replied. 'I can follow that. But is that it? What else do we need?'

'We shall come onto that in a moment,' Tom replied. 'For now I just want you to think about what we have done.

'Just like in our example of the forest and the trees, you have calculated the total cost of a cup of coffee by looking at each of the ingredients that goes into it. You had to use some simple mathematics to handle the different quantities involved, but I'm sure that you will all agree that it is really only a matter of applying common sense in a logical, step by step approach.'

Tom glanced at the clock above the door and saw that it was time to finish the lesson. He walked over to his desk and sat down. Folding his arms on the desk, he leant forward and looked earnestly at the class.

'Once again, this is an example where most of the information and knowledge for our calculations has come from you, not from me. You have done the thinking and calculating bits. All that I have done is to guide you in your thinking and then tell you the words that a businessman or accountant would use for these calculations.

'Let's finish the lesson by summarising all of this into the Direct Costs Budget using our budgeted annual sales.'

Tom wrote the following calculations on the board:

DIRECT COSTS BUDGET			
Coffee	4,800 cups x £0.05	=	£ 240.00
Filters	4,800 x £0.04	=	£ 192.00
Milk	4,800 x £0.03	=	£ 144.00
Sugar	4,800 x £0.02	=	£ 96.00
	Total direct costs	=	£ 672.00

Concepts

DIRECT COSTS, VARIABLE COSTS

These costs are directly related to the level of production or output. If production levels halve or double, these costs will similarly halve or double. Typical examples are fabric in making clothes, or paper in printing books.

10

Indirect Costs

At the start of the next lesson, Tom waited for the level of talking and noise to die down before standing up to speak. 'Ladies and gentlemen,' he began, 'let's now talk about the other costs in our proposed coffee business.'

Turning to Gill, he asked, 'Gill, you mentioned buying a coffee machine last time. How much is it likely to cost?'

Gill opened her bag and pulled out a catalogue from a discount hardware store. 'This is the cheapest place to buy a coffee machine, but we are going to need to buy two so that we can make enough cups for everyone. There is a machine costing £40 that makes eight cups per filling so if we buy two machines there will be no problem.'

'OK,' replied Tom. 'We now know the cost of buying the coffee machines and at our last meeting we calculated the direct cost per cup of coffee. Is that all of the costs or can anyone think of anything else we shall have to buy or pay for?'

'What about the electricity we shall use?' called a voice from the back of the class.

'Yes,' said Tom, 'anything else?'

'What about cups?'

'Who is going to do the washing up?'

'Who is going to drive to the local supermarket to buy the ingredients every few days?'

The next ten minutes was taken up with a discussion of how these points would be sorted out. The general feeling was that no one wanted the job of washing up regularly or driving to the supermarket to buy the ingredients.

'I was thinking along very similar lines to you as well,' said Tom, 'so last night I had a word with the college caretaker, Mr Simpson, about this. He said that he would be prepared to do the washing up and collect the ingredients if we pay him £5 per week. He also said that we shall have to pay £10 per quarter to cover the electricity we use, but this will also allow us to use the college's cups.'

Tom then picked up a pen and wrote on the board:

Caretaker's wages	=	**£ 5 per week**
Electricity	=	**£ 10 per quarter**
Purchase coffee machines	=	**£ 40 x 2 machines**

Turning round to face the class, he asked, 'How shall we deal with these costs? How do they affect the cost of each cup of coffee?'

At first no-one answered. Then a young man in the second row said, 'I don't think you can answer that immediately. Surely it depends on how many cups of coffee you make.'

'Well done,' replied Tom. 'You have just hit on another important point. Our costs for the caretaker and the electricity are not going to alter.

'We shall pay the same amount irrespective of how many cups of coffee we make. They have been agreed at £5 per week for the caretaker and £10 per quarter for the electricity. They are fixed at those levels. In business terms we call them Fixed Costs, Overhead Costs or Indirect Costs.'

'What about the purchase of the coffee machine itself?' asked Mike, the local government officer. 'Is that also an Indirect Cost?'

'Good question,' responded Tom. 'Clearly it is not a direct cost, but neither can we really call it an indirect cost. It is a one-off purchase that we make at the start of the business and which will be used in the business for several years before it wears out. We call it a 'Fixed Asset', and treat it in a special way as you will see later on.'

Tom then wrote on the board:

INDIRECT COSTS BUDGET

Electricity	£ 10 x 4 quarters	=	£ 40.00
Caretaker's wages	£ 5 x 40 weeks	=	£ 200.00
	Annual Indirect Costs	=	£ 240.00

FIXED ASSETS BUDGET

Coffee machines: £ 40 x 2   =   £ 80.00

Concepts

FIXED COSTS, OVERHEAD COSTS, INDIRECT COSTS

These terms all refer to costs which do not vary directly with the level of activity or output in a business.

Typical examples of Fixed or Overhead Costs are rent, rates and head office management salaries.

The term Indirect Cost is more usually used when referring to a fixed cost that is closer to the production process, such as maintenance costs and factory management wages.

SEMI-VARIABLE COSTS, SEMI-FIXED COSTS

This refers to costs that contain both a fixed and variable component. Hourly paid wages are often described in this category as they may contain a guaranteed basic element which is paid whatever the level of work done, together with a variable element paid at overtime premium rates for extra work done.

FIXED ASSETS

This term covers items or property owned and used by the business such as buildings, machinery and cars. They are necessary for the business to produce its product or service, but are not directly consumed or used up in the process. They have a life of several years and are recorded in the books of accounts in a 'Fixed Asset Register' grouped into appropriate categories depending upon their expected useful lives.

11

Depreciation

'This is where the fun bit starts,' exclaimed Tom at the beginning of the next lesson.

Fun? How could all these numbers and calculations be fun? Tom could see the expressions of doubt on nearly everyone's face.

'Oh yes,' he chuckled, 'this is the fun bit as it is now that we begin to see whether we have the beginnings of a real business or if it is just a pipe-dream.

'Now, think back to Mike selling me his newspaper. Do you remember that I paid him £1 for a newspaper that had cost him 40 pence? So he made a profit of 60 pence, right? Remember, profit equals sales less costs, and a business needs to make profits to survive.

'So, let's put it all together for our proposed coffee business and see if it has real potential to work or if it would simply lose money.'

Tom turned to the board and wrote:

COFFEE BUSINESS

Budget for 12 months

SALES BUDGET (p35)		£ 960.00

Deduct :

DIRECT COSTS BUDGET (p40)

Coffee	£ 240.00	
Filters	£ 192.00	
Milk	£ 144.00	
Sugar	£ 96.00	
		£ 672.00

Deduct :

INDIRECT COSTS BUDGET (p43)

Electricity	£ 40.00	
Caretaker's wages	£ 200.00	
		£ 240.00

Deduct :

FIXED ASSETS BUDGET (p49)

Coffee machines		£ 80.00
LOSS		£ (32.00)

As Tom wrote the last line, he added, 'Note that a loss, or negative number, can be shown in brackets, in red ink, or with a minus sign. The most commonly used symbol is the brackets which we have used here.'

Turning to face the class, he asked, 'Well, what do you think? Is this proposed business a good idea or not?'

'No way,' called a voice from the back of the room. 'It's showing a loss so it's not worth going ahead with.'

Several people in the room nodded in agreement with this comment.

Tom sat down and removed his glasses. He pulled a clean, white handkerchief from his jacket pocket and carefully polished them. Putting them back on, he asked the question to the whole class, 'Does everyone agree with this? Is everybody happy with the calculations?'

To her own surprise, Kim, the apprentice hairdresser who was normally shy, held up her hand.

'Yes, Kim?' asked Tom.

Nervously, and afraid of making a fool of herself in front of everyone, Kim spoke up. 'It seems to me that it adds up correctly, but I'm wondering about the numbers.'

'Go on,' Tom encouraged.

'Well, the calculation looks all right as far as it goes, but what about the next year? It wouldn't be the same then, would it?'

Tom nodded in agreement.

'I mean, you wouldn't have the cost of the coffee machines in the next year would you? They've been paid for in the first year.'

'That's right,' said Tom, 'so what would that do to the bottom line in the second year?'

Kim looked at the board for a moment before replying. 'We would take off the Fixed Assets Budget and so the bottom line would be a profit of £48. That means that the business is worth doing in the second year.'

'Thank you,' said Tom. 'What you have said is exactly right and it looks like we have a bit of a dilemma.

'Here is a business that will make profits in its second year, but in its first year it will make a loss, and it's all because of that Fixed

Assets Budget. Does that seem sensible or logical?'

Feeling more confident now, Kim replied, 'How about spreading the Fixed Assets Budget across both years? In other words, divide the £80 cost by 2 and charge £40 in each year.'

'Why only two years?' said the girl sitting behind Kim. 'I've got a coffee machine at home that is still going strong after five years.'

'This is good, very good,' interrupted Tom. 'You are on the right track, but as we haven't got much longer in this lesson I'd like to help you along here.

'What you've correctly realised is that the cost of the coffee machines, or Fixed Asset Budget, is a strange item.

'The way we handle it is to make an estimate of the life of the asset and then to spread the cost over that life.

'If you think that the coffee machines will last two years we will charge £40 per year over those two years.

'If you think that they will last, say, ten years we will charge £8 per year over ten years.

'The charge we make in each year is called 'Depreciation', and it is meant to represent a measure of how much of the asset's value has been used up in a particular year.

'For some strange reason, I find that many students struggle with the idea of depreciation. You see, it is not the same thing as cash expenditure in a particular year. It represents a single cash expenditure charged over several years.'

Tom stopped at this point to look at the class. He knew that this last sentence would confuse some people. Deciding that no one looked totally lost or confused, he continued.

'The one example of depreciation that most people seem to grasp easily enough is that of a motor car.

'Suppose you buy a car for £12,000, and then three years later you might sell it for, say, £5,000. This means that over the three years there has been depreciation of £7,000.

'Of course, the only money that you would have paid out was the initial £12,000. You don't 'pay' depreciation after buying the car.

'It's also worth mentioning a couple of points here. First of all, depreciation isn't necessarily always the same each year. If you consider the second-hand value of the car at the end of each year it might look as follows.'

Tom wrote on the board:

EXAMPLE DEPRECIATION - MOTOR CAR

	Initial value (cost) £ 12,000
Depreciation In Year 1 £ 4,000	Value after 1 year £ 8,000
Depreciation In Year 2 £ 2,000	Value after 2 years £ 6,000
Depreciation In Year 3 £ 1,000	Value after 3 years £ 5,000
Total Depreciation £ 7,000	

'Secondly,' he continued, 'depreciation does not necessarily assume that the asset is fully used up or worn out. As in the case of the car, it can have what we call a 'residual value'.'

Allowing these points to sink in, Tom then asked for suggestions for how to treat depreciation on the coffee machines. The first person to speak was Tony, the retired Army officer.

'Look,' he said, with a confidence gained after many years of military leadership, 'we are all here for three years and I don't suppose the coffee machines will be worn out by then. They cost £40 now, but I'm sure that we could sell them at the end of the three years for £10 each. Why don't we keep it simple by saying that we charge the total loss in value of £60 for the two machines at a flat rate of £20 depreciation per year?'

Perhaps it was Tony's decisive and confident way of speaking, or maybe the logic of his proposal, but no-one spoke or disagreed.

'Very well,' said Tom, 'I think we can all go along with that, so the annual depreciation charge is agreed at £20.

'Let's now restate our Year 1 budget and see how it looks.'

COFFEE BUSINESS

Budget for 12 months

SALES BUDGET		**£ 960.00**

Deduct :

DIRECT COSTS BUDGET

Coffee	£ 240.00	
Filters	£ 192.00	
Milk	£ 144.00	
Sugar	£ 96.00	
		£ 672.00

Deduct :

INDIRECT COSTS BUDGET

Electricity	£ 40.00	
Caretaker's wages	£ 200.00	
Depreciation	£ 20.00	
		£ 260.00

PROFIT		**£ 28.00**

Concepts

DEPRECIATION, NET BOOK VALUE

Depreciation is the term used to describe the wearing out of a fixed asset over a period of time, usually several years. This is recognised in the accounts of a business by spreading the cost of the asset over several years rather than charging it all in the year that it is purchased.

The amount that it is estimated to have worn out in a particular year is deducted from the profit of the year as a 'depreciation charge' and the value of the asset after deducting depreciation is recorded in the books of account as the 'net book value' of the fixed asset.

There are various mathematical accounting methods for calculating depreciation charges. They are used to reflect the type of fixed asset and the rate at which it wears out or reduces in value over its estimated useful life. In all cases, however, depreciation is simply a method of spreading the cost of the asset over several accounting years.

12

The Profit and Loss Account

The budget was still on the board at the start of the next lesson. Tom picked up a cloth and began to wipe out a few of the words on it. He then wrote in a few different words, but did not change any of the numbers. When he had finished, the budget read:

COFFEE BUSINESS

**Budgeted Profit and Loss Account
for the year to 31st December 200_**

	£	£
TURNOVER		**960**
COST OF GOODS SOLD		
Materials: Coffee	240	
Filters	192	
Milk	144	
Sugar	96	
		672
GROSS PROFIT		**288**
OVERHEAD COSTS		
Electricity	40	
Caretaker's wages	200	
Depreciation	20	
		260
NET PROFIT		**28**

'There!' he exclaimed triumphantly, 'now we have come full circle!'

'Full circle? What do you mean?' asked Gill.

'Well,' Tom replied, 'what you have there is a Budgeted Profit and

Loss Account that you might expect to see for a typical business. I've changed a few words here and there, but none of the numbers or calculations has changed.'

'Yes, I can see that and I recognise and understand those numbers. But I still don't see what you mean by coming full circle.'

Tom smiled at her. 'Gill, it's not so long ago that I wrote something rather similar on the board and then asked you to go away and read textbooks on the subject. That's when you told me that it was all a load of jargon and nonsense. If my memory serves me correctly, you also said that it was lots of complicated words, fancy mathematics and no explanations. Am I right?'

Gill nodded her head in agreement, feeling both amused and embarrassed at what she had said. 'Yes, but the point is that you have made it all seem so simple and obvious.'

'Thank you for that compliment,' Tom replied, 'but it is you that have done the hard work, not me. I have simply guided you.

'Remember the example of the trees and the forest? Most textbooks simply put a forest under your nose and then try to explain it. What we have done is to build the forest on a tree-by-tree basis.

'What is more, by choosing the coffee machine, we are using 'trees' that you can understand and relate to.'

Tom was pleased to see several heads nodding in agreement.

'I think that we are now all agreed on one thing,' he continued. 'Our proposed coffee business looks good. Not only can we get the better coffee we want, but we know that the business stands a very good chance of making a modest profit.'

Tidying the papers on his desk, he said, 'A while ago we introduced the idea of the Profit Forecast. What you have now seen is how to put it all together and to present it in the standard business format more commonly known as the Budgeted Profit and Loss Account.

'Congratulations, everyone! You have now mastered the most important financial procedure in planning any sort of business.'

Concepts

PROFIT AND LOSS ACCOUNT

Often referred to as the 'P & L Account,' this is the most important financial statement in any business. It provides a statement of the total income (i.e. 'how much money came in') less all of the costs of the business (i.e. 'where the money was spent') for the accounting period. The difference between the income and costs is the profit or loss for the period.

The term Profit & Loss Account can be confusing. The account can never show a profit AND loss for the same accounting period. The term 'Income & Expenditure Account' which is sometimes used to describe the same financial statement is perhaps less confusing.

Profit & Loss accounts also contain various accounting terms as shown below.

TURNOVER

This term is often used instead of 'Sales' but has the same meaning and is the total income of the business generated from its sale of goods or services in the accounting period. It does not include items such as discounts given to customers or Value Added Tax which, although included in the sales price to customers, are not income to the business.

COST OF GOODS SOLD

Where a business holds stocks of goods that are

subsequently used in manufacturing or sold to customers, the value of the goods sold in a particular period is not necessarily the same as the value of goods purchased in the period. This is reflected in the level of stocks either rising or falling in the period.

For example, if a business purchases 10 tins of paint and sells 8 tins in the period, its stocks will increase by 2 tins. Although the business has paid for 10 tins, the cost of goods sold will be the cost of 8 tins.

The accounting formula to calculate the cost of goods sold is:

Cost of goods sold =   opening stock
+ purchases
– closing stock

GROSS PROFIT

This is the measure of profit calculated by deducting the Cost Of Goods Sold from the Turnover. It shows the profit of the business before taking into account the Overhead Costs.

NET PROFIT, THE BOTTOM LINE

Net Profit is sometimes referred to as 'The Bottom Line'. It is calculated by deducting the Overhead Costs from the Gross Profit. This calculation includes all costs incurred by the business and consequently Net Profit is the yardstick by which the financial success of the business is measured.

13

What If?

Pleased with the positive progress that the class was now making, Tom picked up a pen and his pocket calculator. He then added a percentage column to the right hand side:

.

COFFEE BUSINESS

**Budgeted Profit and Loss Account
for the year to 31st December 200_**

	£	£	%
TURNOVER		960	
COST OF GOODS SOLD			
Materials: Coffee	240		25
Filters	192		20
Milk	144		15
Sugar	96		10
		672	70
GROSS PROFIT		288	30
OVERHEAD COSTS			
Electricity	40		4
Caretaker's wages	200		21
Depreciation	20		2
		260	27
NET PROFIT		28	3

'I'm calculating a series of percentages expressed in terms of the Turnover,' said Tom. 'There are two reasons for showing you this.

'First of all, I want you to notice the Gross Profit expressed as 30% of Turnover. This is what people in business, particularly those involved in sales activities, mean when they say 'I'm making 30% on that business'. I'm sure that you've all heard phrases like that before, but now you can see exactly what it means. Putting it another way, for every £1 of sales, 30 pence is kept in the business as Gross Profit.'

Tom paused to allow people to take note of this important point.

'The second point I want to introduce to you is the idea of 'Sensitivity Analysis'. This is an area that I find particularly interesting as it can have dramatic implications for a business. The strange thing is, though, many business people often seem unaware of it or do not use it to their advantage.

'The idea of sensitivity analysis is to see how sensitive the Net Profit is to a change in any one or more aspects of the business. This is also sometimes known as playing 'what if?' games.

'Let's start by looking at the Net Profit at 3% of Turnover. Compare it with the other percentages. You can see the lines showing much higher percentages, like the coffee and caretaker's wages. A very small change in any of the high percentage numbers would have a dramatic effect on the Net Profit.

'For example, suppose the price of coffee were to halve. What would happen? Our cost of coffee would fall to £120.00, or 12%, and the Net Profit would rise to £148, or 15%.

'But what if we were able to halve the cost of the electricity? The effect would be far less dramatic. The cost would fall to £20, or 2%, causing the Net Profit to rise to £48, or 5%.'

Tom noticed that several people in the room had picked up their pocket calculators and were tapping in numbers, obviously experimenting in the way he had shown them.

'The extraordinary thing,' Tom continued, 'is that people in business often ignore this sensitivity analysis and focus their attention on less important matters. We may even be guilty of this ourselves if we are not careful.'

'Why do think that?' asked Tony.

'Well,' Tom replied, 'if we want to cut costs, we may look at those items that we think are easiest to control. For example, we may regard the electricity charge as a cost that we might be able to renegotiate with the college, whilst the cost of coffee is fixed by the supermarket.

I think we can all see, however, that our energies would be better applied in trying to find a cheaper source of coffee.'

'Isn't that obvious, though?' asked Tony.

'Yes, with this approach it probably is,' replied Tom, 'but you would be surprised how often this is missed by all types of business and organisation.

'The biggest surprise of all, though, is when we look at the Turnover.'

Tom pointed to the Turnover line on the board and then to the Gross Profit line.

'Remember what we said a minute ago about the 30% margin. That means that for every extra £1 of sales we have to spend 70 pence on the ingredients leaving only 30 pence as Gross Profit. In other words, 70% of the profit effect of the extra sale is lost due to the cost of goods sold effect.'

Tom paused to let everyone think about this. When he felt confident that they understood it, he added, 'And that is why it is sometimes far better in business to spend a little effort on controlling the costs rather than a lot of effort trying to increase the Turnover.

'Too often in business, people lose sight of the relationship between Turnover and Profit. That's why there is a wise old saying, "Turnover is vanity, Profit is sanity".'

Concepts

SENSITIVITY ANALYSIS, FINANCIAL MODELS

This is a means of testing the outcome of a plan or budget. Changes are made to estimates of the inputs to see how a small change in an input will affect the final output.

In a business plan or budget, typical inputs to examine would be expected sales demand, price levels, costs, quantities and time scales. A small change in each of these inputs could be examined to see the effect on Net Profit. If a small change produces a large change in Net Profit, the Net Profit is very sensitive to changes in that particular input. Consequently, the financial viability of the business is similarly very sensitive to changes in that particular input.

With the widespread use of computers and spreadsheets, many businesses produce detailed budgets (or 'financial models') that allow sensitivity analysis to be carried out very quickly and accurately as the computer can perform the necessary mathematics very rapidly and produce high quality printed results.

14

The Budget Holder

'You've certainly made all of that much easier to understand,' said Gill enthusiastically, 'but I'm not entirely clear how it relates to me, working in a hospital.'

'Or me, working in the Police,' added Mike.

'Fair comment,' responded Tom. 'Let's spend a short while thinking about how it relates to you all.'

As he looked round the room his gaze fell upon Kim. 'Kim, you must be one of the most obvious examples of someone who can immediately appreciate the need and benefit of what we are looking at. After all, right at the beginning you told us that you want to set up your own hairdressing business. Just think how helpful all of this will be for you.

'For a start, how many customers can you cut and shampoo in a day? How much will you charge for each hairdo or treatment?

'What will it cost for the various shampoos, lotions, towels and so on? How many types of scissors will you need, and how long will they last?

'Can you do all of the work on your own? Will you need to hire staff? What about premises? What about the special fittings like washbasins and mirrors?'

Kim nodded. 'Yes, those are all things that I need to think about, and in a funny way your Budgeted Profit and Loss Account will help me with more than just the numbers. You see, it helps me to get all of my thoughts into a logical order. It takes a lot of the confusion out of it.'

'Thank you for that vote of confidence,' Tom laughed. 'I think that you will all agree that Kim's situation is easy to understand. And why is that?'

Before anyone could attempt to answer, he continued, 'It's all a question of scale or size of the business. We can all picture a hairdressing business as it can be run by as little as just one person. But when it comes to large organisations, like large or multi-national companies, the National Health Service, the Police or local government, we are talking about a completely different scale of operation.

'Make no mistake, though, the underlying principles are just the same. They are all organisations that have to control their finances, and they do this by looking at their income and costs.'

He looked towards Gill.

'Gill, what financial responsibilities have they given you at your Hospital Trust?'

'As a nurse manager, I have been told that next year I shall be responsible for the budget for my ward. Having said that, I really don't see where items like Turnover come into it for me.'

'I don't suppose you will have anything to do with Turnover,' replied Tom. 'Almost certainly, you will concentrate on looking at the costs of running the ward. I imagine that you will be responsible for looking at two main categories of cost, your staff costs and the materials costs.'

Gill nodded in agreement.

'To calculate your staff costs, you will need to look at the number of nurses, their grades, and probably the amount of overtime they are expected to work. Am I right?'

'Yes, it all sounds depressingly familiar,' laughed Gill.

'And on the materials, would I be right in thinking that you look at costs for laundry, drugs, dressings and so on?'

'Yes, these are all items I shall be having to look at,' replied Gill, 'and I suppose we can consider these using your Direct Costs and Indirect Costs approach.'

'Exactly right,' replied Tom. 'You are in a situation where you will be responsible for part of the hospital's finances on the cost side. Make no mistake, though, someone somewhere will be putting it all together to examine the hospital's overall financial position The senior management will be concerned with the Profit and Loss Account for the hospital, although it will almost certainly be called the 'Income and Expenditure Account'. It's the same thing really, but the hospital is more likely to use this description, together with 'surplus' or 'deficit'. This is because its main concern is to match expenditure to income rather than to make a profit.

'You are not responsible for the Turnover, or perhaps it would be more appropriate to say Income, of the hospital. But, as the person who authorises staff levels and overtime working, and who signs the orders for the items used on the ward, you are the best person to control expenditure on the ward.

'Your ward is called a 'Cost Centre' as it is a clearly defined area where expenditure takes place. The hospital allocates a budget to the ward, or Cost Centre, and expects you as the manager in charge, or 'Budget Holder', to make sure that expenditure incurred during the year is not allowed to exceed the budgeted amount, without very good reason. This management technique is known as 'Budgetary Control'.

'As we said some time ago, the spread of PCs and computing power means that much more financial information can be produced at, shall we say, the 'grass roots' level in large organisations like the NHS. So, when funds are limited and the NHS has to live within its total income, it makes sense to give financial information to the people actually spending money. After all, if they are held responsible for ensuring that it is spent wisely, they are in the best position to ensure that unnecessary expenditure and wastage is cut out. That is why budgetary control is being used to an increasing extent in all organisations and why so many of you are now expected to be budget holders with financial responsibilities.'

'When you put it like that,' said Gill, 'I begin to see how it all fits in. I suppose it is all part of a large jigsaw. Yes, and to complete a jigsaw you need all of the pieces. That makes my small contribution to the overall financial health of the hospital all the more important, doesn't it?'

She smiled triumphantly.

Concepts

COST CENTRE

An area of the business or organisation where costs can be identified and controlled by the manager in charge of that area. Often the cost centre is a particular department or function, but in a manufacturing environment, it can also be a group of machines or a particular process.

BUDGET HOLDER, BUDGET CENTRE

A budget holder is the person or manager in charge of a department or cost centre for which a budget is prepared ('Budget Centre'). The budget holder is normally involved in preparing the budget and will be held responsible for ensuring that the financial results of the department are acceptably close to the budgeted levels.

BUDGETARY CONTROL, BUDGET STATEMENTS

Budgetary Control is the term given to controlling a business through a clearly defined structure of budgets, budget centres and budget holders. Senior management in the organisation will be responsible for ensuring that the budgeted results are achieved for the overall organisation, whilst individual budget holders are held responsible for specific areas and departments in the business.

Budgets are normally set before the start of the financial year with involvement from all relevant managers. At regular intervals during the financial year, normally monthly, 'Budget Statements' are prepared and distributed to all budget holders showing the actual results achieved against the budgeted level. This identifies areas where any corrective actions may need to be taken to ensure that the business achieves its targets for the year.

15

The Cash Flow Forecast

Tom felt pleased with the progress the class was making. Using the coffee business as a model to teach the basic principles of finance and accounting was working well. Although they had only stumbled on the idea by chance, following Gill's complaints, the whole class had adopted the idea and were keen to use it as a model to learn. Now it was time to move on and to see if they could actually set up the business and run it.

'How much is it going to cost to set up our coffee business?' he asked.

'£80 to buy the 2 coffee machines,' volunteered a voice from a seat near the window.

'What about paying for the coffee and other ingredients?' said another voice.

'When do we pay the caretaker?' said someone else.

Tom raised his hand before any further suggestions could be called out. 'Thank you, those are all valid points,' he said. 'This is where I want to introduce the idea of the 'Cash Flow Forecast'.

'I'm sure that you have come across the expression 'cash flow' before, but here is an opportunity to see what it means and why it is so important.

'Cash flow is all about seeing when actual cash, or money, comes into and goes out of the business. As you may be aware, the time of receipt of bills for a particular period and the time of payment do not necessarily coincide.

'For example, you may receive an electricity bill for the three month period of January to March, but you may not actually pay it until late in April or perhaps early May. In other words, the cash is paid some considerable time after the charge has been incurred.

'Working out the cash flow implications at the start of a business tells you just exactly how much cash will be needed to start the business and keep it going.'

Tom then turned to the board and copied down the now familiar Budgeted Profit and Loss Account. He then added a column headed 'Start Up', followed by four 'Quarterly' columns.

'Cash flow forecasts can be as simple or as complicated as you like. As you know, money comes in and is paid out on a daily basis in most businesses. So we could, in theory at least, produce a cash flow forecast predicting cash flows on a daily basis for the year ahead.

'I think you will agree, however, that we haven't got the time, board space or crystal ball forecasting powers to make that worthwhile. Instead, let's do what many businesses do, and that is to use a monthly or quarterly forecast. For our purposes I think that a quarterly forecast will do nicely.'

At that moment his pen ran out of ink. He carefully selected a replacement pen before continuing.

'Let's think about the Turnover first of all. Can someone comment on this please?'

'I reckon that everyone should pay each time they buy their coffee,' said Rajiv, the computer salesman.

'Fair enough,' replied Tom. 'So how much money can we expect to collect by the end of Quarter 1?'

'Presumably exactly one quarter of the full year amount,' Rajiv replied.

'And the next quarter?'

'Same again.'

Tom divided the full year total Turnover by 4, to arrive at £240 per quarter. He wrote this into the Cash Flow Forecast. Everyone noticed that he left the Start-up column blank:

COFFEE BUSINESS

Budgeted Profit and Loss Account
for the year to 31st December 200_

	£	£	Start-up	Q1	Q2	Q3	Q4
TURNOVER		**960**		**240**	**240**	**240**	**240**
COST OF GOODS SOLD							
Materials: Coffee	**240**						
Filters	**192**						
Milk	**144**						
Sugar	**96**						
		672					
GROSS PROFIT		**288**					
OVERHEAD COSTS							
Electricity	**40**						
Caretaker's wages	**200**						
Depreciation	**20**						
		260					
NET PROFIT		**28**					

'Let's now look at the ingredients,' he said. 'What do you think, Rajiv. Divide into equal quarters as we did for the Turnover?'

Rajiv nodded his head in agreement, and Tom wrote on the board:

COFFEE BUSINESS

Budgeted Profit and Loss Account
for the year to 31st December 200_

	£	£	Start-up	Q1	Q2	Q3	Q4
TURNOVER		960		240	240	240	240
COST OF GOODS SOLD							
Materials: Coffee	240			60	60	60	60
Filters	192			48	48	48	48
Milk	144			36	36	36	36
Sugar	96			24	24	24	24
		672					
GROSS PROFIT		288					
OVERHEAD COSTS							
Electricity	40						
Caretaker's wages	200						
Depreciation	20						
		260					
NET PROFIT		28					

As Tom finished writing he asked, 'Before we carry on further, can anyone spot what is missing?'

'Is it the Start-Up column?' a voice volunteered.

'Exactly right. Before we can make any coffee to sell we have got to go out and stock up with the necessary ingredients.' He paused and then added, 'Note that I have just used the word 'stock'.

'You see, not only have we got to buy and pay for the ingredients that will actually be used in making the cups of coffee, but we have also got to keep a stock of ingredients in hand. These have to be paid for as well at the outset.'

To reinforce the point he added, 'It's just like cooking a meal at home. Some of the ingredients will come from stocks in the pantry. These have to be bought and paid for before preparing the meal.'

He continued with the analogy of the pantry to explain the next point.

'Some of you will no doubt have well stocked pantries at home. Others will keep very little. The full pantries require money to set up and run the risk of foodstuffs becoming stale, whilst the poorly stocked pantries may not have enough of a crucial ingredient just when it is needed.

'There is no precise way of determining the most appropriate level, it is largely a matter of good judgement. And so it is in business.

'I suggest, however, that in our coffee business we should buy at least enough ingredients to cover the first week. As you will recall, our Sales Plan shows weekly sales of 120 cups of coffee. Let's take another look at our Cost Of Ingredients.'

Tom turned to write on the board :

COST OF INGREDIENTS

Coffee   £ 2.50 per box – makes 50 cups = £ 0.05 per cup

Filters   £ 2.00 per box – makes 50 cups = £ 0.04 per cup

Milk   £ 0.36 per pint – makes 12 cups = £ 0.03 per cup

Sugar   £ 0.80 per bag – makes 40 cups = £ 0.02 per cup
_____
Total Cost Of Ingredients   = £ 0.14 per cup

'Right,' he continued, 'this is our starting point to calculate how much initial stock of ingredients we shall require. Based on the figure of 120 cups of coffee in the first week we shall need to set up with the following quantities.'

Tom then altered the Cost of Ingredients to read as follows:

START UP INGREDIENTS REQUIRED							
To make at least 120 cups							
Coffee	£ 2.50 per box (50 cups)	=	3 boxes	=	£ 7.50
Filters	£ 2.00 per box (50 cups)	=	3 boxes	=	£ 6.00
Milk	£ 0.36 per pint (12 cups)	=	10 pints	=	£ 3.60
Sugar	£ 0.80 per bag (40 cups)	=	3 bags	=	£ 2.40
			Total	=	£ 19.50

'As you will appreciate,' Tom continued, 'these are estimates and not precise calculations. There is no advantage in working to the nearest penny in the cash flow forecast, so we can round the numbers to the nearest £ to show ingredients totalling £20 and put them in the Start Up column like this.'

COFFEE BUSINESS

Budgeted Profit and Loss Account
for the year to 31st December 200_

	£	£	Start-up	Q1	Q2	Q3	Q4
TURNOVER		960		240	240	240	240
COST OF GOODS SOLD							
Materials: Coffee	240		8	60	60	60	60
Filters	192		6	48	48	48	48
Milk	144		4	36	36	36	36
Sugar	96		2	24	24	24	24
		672					
GROSS PROFIT		288					
OVERHEAD COSTS							
Electricity	40						
Caretaker's wages	200						
Depreciation	20						
		260					
NET PROFIT		28					

Tom then repeated this process with the Overhead Costs. He had agreed with the college that the contribution to the electricity should be paid quarterly in arrears, so the charge for the first quarter would not be paid until the second quarter. The caretaker's wages, however, were to be paid at the end of each month.

COFFEE BUSINESS

Budgeted Profit and Loss Account
for the year to 31st December 200_

	£	£	Start-up	Q1	Q2	Q3	Q4
TURNOVER		960		240	240	240	240
COST OF GOODS SOLD							
Materials: Coffee	240		8	60	60	60	60
Filters	192		6	48	48	48	48
Milk	144		4	36	36	36	36
Sugar	96		2	24	24	24	24
		672					
GROSS PROFIT		288					
OVERHEAD COSTS							
Electricity	40				10	10	10
Caretaker's wages	200			50	50	50	50
Depreciation	20						
		260					
NET PROFIT		28					

'What about depreciation?' asked Tom.

'Same thing again. Divide by 4,' answered someone.

'Does everyone agree with that?' asked Tom.

Mike spoke up at this moment.

'Surely we are not actually paying out cash for depreciation. The depreciation is simply how we have chosen to spread the cost of buying the coffee machines in the first place.'

Tom looked at Mike. 'You are dead right, Mike, and I like the way you put that, 'spreading the cost of buying the coffee machines in the first place'. How about substituting the words 'first place' with 'Start-Up'?'

Mike looked puzzled for a minute, but it suddenly dawned on him.

'So what we need to do,' he said, 'is to put the £80 cost of the coffee machines in the Start-Up column and then ignore the depreciation.'

'Mike, well done, that is exactly right. And if anyone is puzzled by that, think again about our example of buying and charging depreciation on a car.'

Tom then added the purchase cost of the coffee machines on the board:

COFFEE BUSINESS

Budgeted Profit and Loss Account
for the year to 31st December 200_

	£	£	Start-up	Q1	Q2	Q3	Q4
TURNOVER		960		240	240	240	240
COST OF GOODS SOLD							
Materials: Coffee	240		8	60	60	60	60
Filters	192		6	48	48	48	48
Milk	144		4	36	36	36	36
Sugar	96		2	24	24	24	24
		672					
GROSS PROFIT		288					
OVERHEAD COSTS							
Electricity	40				10	10	10
Caretaker's wages	200			50	50	50	50
Depreciation	20						
		260					
COFFEE MACHINES			**80**				
NET PROFIT		28					

He then placed brackets around all of the cost items to show that they would represent cash leaving the business, or 'negative cash flow' items. At the bottom of the workings he added another line called 'Net

(Cash Out) / Cash In'. Finally, he deleted unnecessary lines, changed the heading, and then added up the columns:

COFFEE BUSINESS

Cash Flow Forecast
for the year to 31st December 200_

	Start-up	Q1	Q2	Q3	Q4
RECEIPTS FROM SALES		240	240	240	240
TOTAL CASH IN		240	240	240	240
PURCHASES					
Materials: Coffee	(8)	(60)	(60)	(60)	(60)
Filters	(6)	(48)	(48)	(48)	(48)
Milk	(4)	(36)	(36)	(36)	(36)
Sugar	(2)	(24)	(24)	(24)	(24)
OVERHEAD COSTS					
Electricity			(10)	(10)	(10)
Caretaker's wages		(50)	(50)	(50)	(50)
COFFEE MACHINES	(80)				
TOTAL CASH OUT	(100)	(218)	(228)	(228)	(228)
NET (CASH OUT)/CASH IN	(100)	22	12	12	12
CUMULATIVE (CASH OUT)/CASH IN	(100)	(78)	(66)	(54)	(42)

Concepts

CASH FLOW FORECAST

This is a statement which shows the anticipated cash receipts and payments based on a budgeted Profit & Loss Account. It recognises the fact that many business transactions are based on credit and the payment for goods and services does not necessarily coincide with the particular transaction.

It also highlights the fact that the cash payment for fixed assets will normally be required at the time of purchase whereas the useful life of the asset and corresponding depreciation will be spread over several years. Consequently, the Cash Flow Forecast does not include depreciation as shown in the Profit & Loss Account.

For example, a motor-car purchased for cash will appear in the Cash Flow Forecast of just the year of purchase, whilst its depreciation charge will be spread across several subsequent years' Profit & Loss Accounts.

Cash Flow Forecasts are important in assessing the amount of cash, or the extent of a bank overdraft, that a business may require.

16

Funding the Business

'If you all now look at the bottom line of our Cash Flow Forecast you will see that the Start-Up cash out totals to £100.'

Tom pointed to the relevant figure. Moving his hand along to the right he then added, 'As you can see this figure reduces as the year goes on and the cumulative cash deficit reduces as the business generates profits. It is down to a deficit of £42 by the end of Quarter 4.

'So, to start this business up we need to find 'Sources Of Finance' to cover the initial £100.

'Any volunteers?'

The complete silence that followed this request to provide money was followed by a ripple of laughter.

'I thought as much,' chuckled Tom, 'so let's take a closer look at what this £100 represents before we go any further.'

He sat down at his desk before continuing.

'Whilst no-one wants to provide the £100 required, I am sure that you will agree that this is not a vast sum of money. It is quite possible that we could find someone, somewhere, who could be persuaded to provide this amount.

'It's much the same for any type of business or organisation. The largest organisations like the National Health Service are effectively funded by a single source, the Government. Many very large corporations are owned by larger multinational parent companies, and so are also funded by a single entity. At the other end of the scale, many small businesses are often funded by a single person, the owner, or perhaps a single organisation such as a bank.

'There are many other businesses, however, where several sources of finance are used to fund different aspects of the business. It is this approach that I want to consider for our coffee business and to see if some of you can be persuaded to invest in the business after all.'

More laughter followed Tom's suggestion that he could get some of the class to spend money.

'The first principle that I want to introduce to you is that long-term assets of the business, the Fixed Assets, are often funded by long-term capital, whilst the medium- and short-term assets are funded by medium- and short-term debt.'

Realising that several people were staring at him blankly following this last statement, Tom decided that further explanation was required.

'Put it this way. It's very similar to your own personal finances. If you buy a house, you will normally borrow money from a building society to pay for it over a period of up to 25 years. If you buy a car you may take out a hire purchase agreement or a loan of up to 5 years. If you simply need to pay some bills you will probably ask your bank for an overdraft on your current account. And it is very similar in business.'

Tom stood up and turned to the board. Pointing at the figure of £80 he said, 'These are our Fixed Assets which we can look to fund with long-term debt. The remaining £20 is what we call 'Working Capital'.

'Let's now see if we can attract you to fund the business.'

He turned to face the class.

'First of all, is there anyone here who is prepared to take a small risk to make some money?'

Several people indicated that they would.

'As you know,' Tom continued, 'we are forecasting an annual profit of £28. But let's be honest, it is only a forecast, and in reality we may make more or we may make less, or even nothing at all. Who is prepared to invest, say, £20 for a share of the profits?'

At this point Tony, Mike and Rajiv held up their hands.

'Thank you,' said Tom. 'Here we have 3 people who are prepared to invest a total of £60 in return for a share of the profits. You are what are termed 'Shareholders' as you will own 'Shares' in the business.

We shall talk more about what this means later on.'

Turning to the rest of the class, Tom said, 'Obviously £60 isn't enough. Is no-one else prepared to take a risk and invest?'

'I would be prepared to put some money in,' replied Dave, the local government officer, 'if it wasn't a risk. Say, for example, that I took £30 out of my building society account, I would lose my risk-free interest on that money.'

'Okay,' replied Tom, 'what would it take to persuade you to withdraw your money from the building society and invest it in the business?'

Dave thought for a short while and then replied, 'A rate of interest at least as good as the building society and the confidence to know that my money was safe.'

'Fair enough,' replied Tom. 'Suppose we give you a better rate of interest and a guarantee that if the business fails you can have the coffee machines to keep or sell as you wish?'

'Yes, that sounds acceptable,' replied Dave.

'Thank you, we have just introduced you to the business as a 'Debenture' holder. What this means is that we will guarantee to pay you your agreed rate of interest before the profits are shared out. In addition, we will give you 'Security' by way of what is called a 'Fixed Charge' over the coffee machines. Putting it another way, Dave, think of it like the mortgage on your house. If you fail to keep up your payments to the building society they have a legal right to take ownership of your house which they can sell to get their money back. A mortgage and a Fixed Charge are really the same thing.'

Tom paused to allow the class to make a note of what he had just said.

'Right, we now have £90 of the £100 we need. Can anyone else be persuaded to invest the additional £10?'

No-one said a word.

'All right,' laughed Tom. 'I suppose that this is where I come in, and this is what I propose to do.

'I shall act as a bank to the business and lend the £10. I expect some interest in return, but unlike our three Shareholders I don't expect a share in the profits. What I would like, however, is some sort of security similar to Dave.

'Now, we know that Dave is a Debenture holder and has a charge over the coffee machines. So what security can I have? Does the business own anything else of value?'

'What about all of the ingredients?' suggested Mike.

'Yes, that is a good idea, but we can't exactly put a Fixed Charge over boxes of coffee and bags of sugar that are constantly being used up and then replaced. Just think of all of the paperwork if we created a new Fixed Charge every time we bought a new box of coffee or bag of sugar!'

'Surely you don't need to,' interrupted Mike. 'Couldn't we just issue you with a certificate that says that if the business goes bust you can take whatever ingredients are in the cupboard?'

'Excellent idea, and you have just introduced the concept of the 'Floating Charge'.'

'I have?' replied Mike, feeling rather pleased with himself.

'Yes, a Floating Charge is similar to a Fixed Charge but it does not attach itself to one specific asset. It is said to 'float' over a class of assets, and if the business fails, it effectively attaches itself to those assets. When this happens the Floating Charge is said to have 'crystallised'.

'Let's now look at our total funding structure.'

Tom wrote the following:

PROPOSED FUNDING STRUCTURE

	£	£	Security
SHAREHOLDERS:			
Tony	20		Unsecured
Mike	20		Unsecured
Rajiv	20		Unsecured
		60	
DEBENTURES:			
Dave		30	Fixed Charge
LOAN:			
Tom		10	Floating Charge
TOTAL FUNDING		100	

Concepts

SOURCES OF FINANCE

This refers to the provision of finance to cover the organisation's various monetary requirements. When a business is well established and generating good profits, it can use its own money to meet expenditure and to pay for new assets or expansions. This is referred to as 'internal funding'.

At the outset, however, or if the business wishes to expand more rapidly than it can afford by reinvesting its own profits, it will have to seek external funding or sources of finance. Examples of these are considered in the following definitions.

FIXED CAPITAL, LONG-TERM CAPITAL

This refers to finance provided primarily to pay for the fixed assets and longer-term aspects of the business. Providers of this capital are usually looking for a longer-term involvement with the company and may be owners of the business or banking institutions providing specialist loans.

MEDIUM-TERM, SHORT-TERM DEBT

This refers to finance provided primarily to pay for the shorter-term requirements of the business. For example, company cars may be leased over a period of 3 years, whilst a one-year bank loan might pay for a new machine. Day-to-day cash shortages may be met by use of a bank overdraft facility which is only used when the account becomes temporarily overdrawn.

WORKING CAPITAL

This refers to the money that is required to conduct the day-to-day operations of an organisation. It takes into account the amount of money that is needed to pay for stocks of materials and finished goods and money owed to the business by customers who have not yet paid for their purchases. This is offset by the amounts that are similarly owed by the business to its suppliers.

SHARES, SHAREHOLDERS

Issue of shares is a method of raising long-term capital by a company. The company sells shares (i.e. issues certificates) to people and institutions who are prepared to invest money in the company in the hope of benefiting if the company performs well and produces good profits.

The shareholders of a company are its legal owners and are entitled to a share in its profits.

DEBENTURE

A Debenture is another method of raising long-term capital by a company. It is a special type of long-term loan (typically 10 to 15 years) that provides finance for the company without having to give away any part of the ownership of the business. Holders of debentures are normally paid before net profits are calculated for the benefit of shareholders. In this way it is more secure than shares if the company fails to meet its profit targets.

SECURITY

A term that refers to the protection given to a lender or investor in a business in the event that the business fails to pay agreed interest or to meet the repayments. Where there is a high level of security, there is less risk for the lender and consequently the cost of borrowing money would normally be lower.

FIXED CHARGE

A Fixed Charge is a special form of security or collateral provided to a lender or investor on a specific asset which can be legally claimed in the event of a default. A very common example is a mortgage on property.

FLOATING CHARGE

A Floating Charge is a special form of security or collateral provided to a lender (such as a bank) or investor over a group of assets which can be legally claimed in the event of a default. Unlike a Fixed Charge, the assets in question such as stocks of goods will not be individually identified unless the charge is invoked.

When a Floating Charge is invoked it is said to have 'crystallised' and effectively becomes a Fixed Charge on the assets over which it previously floated.

17

The Structure of the Business

'As you can see, our proposed business is now really beginning to take shape. Our Budgeted Profit and Loss Account indicates that we can expect to make a profit, our Cash Flow Forecast shows us how much funding we shall require, and we have now got the necessary sources of finance. What we must now do is to consider the 'Business Constitution'.'

Tom paused. 'By that I mean that we must think about what our business really is. Does it exist in its own right or does it belong to someone or maybe several people?

'There are four main types of business organisation that I want to describe to you very briefly. They are 'Public Services', 'Limited Companies', 'Partnerships' and 'Sole Traders'.

'No matter which of these business structures you look at, you will see that there are three key elements regarding the constitution.

'Who owns it?

'Who runs it?

'What are the rules governing it?

'If any of you care to go to the law section of your local library, you will see that there are hundreds of books that cover these subjects. Believe me, we could spend all of our time on this course just discussing these different business constitutions. But, I'm pleased to tell you, we shall not be doing that.'

An audible sigh of relief was heard from the class.

'Let me just give you a quick summary of the key points as follows. You are familiar with the many types of **Public Services** such as the NHS, the Police, local authorities, nationalised industries and so on. To a large extent these organisations are all operated in accordance with written rules that are specific to their type of operation. I don't intend to go into these, but please just note that in a financial sense they are all ultimately businesses that have to manage their finances in ways that we have been talking about.'

Nobody raised any questions and so Tom continued to talk about the other types of business.

'The simplest business organisation is the **sole trader**. It is owned and run by the person in charge of it, and there are relatively few rules regarding how it is run. This is the sort of organisation that Kim is most likely to start with if she sets up on her own running a hairdressing salon.

'The next type of business is the **partnership**. Partnerships are traditionally found amongst the so-called 'professions' such as doctors and lawyers. They often arise when more people and more money are needed to run the business. Say, for example, Kim wants to expand her hairdressing business and needs more money for larger premises. One way to do this is to seek a partner who will run the business with her. Again, the rules governing partnerships are not too formal, although there are certain areas of the law that apply to partnerships in certain circumstances.'

Tom paused and walked over to the window. He turned round and continued speaking.

'**Limited companies** are one of the most common forms of business, but I suspect they are the ones that you know least about.

'The idea of a limited company came about in mid-Victorian times when it was realised that the type and size of business that followed the industrial revolution was getting too big for sole traders and partnerships. Above all, these new large businesses needed access to larger amounts of funding or capital.

'The basic problem with a sole trader or partnership is that if the business goes bust and owes money to other people or companies, the individual can be sued for that money. In extreme cases this means that the sole trader or partner can lose his or her home to pay off the debts of the business.'

'Does that mean that I could go bankrupt if my hairdressing salon failed?' asked Kim in alarm.

'Yes, Kim, I'm afraid it does, and that's why you may want to consider running it as a limited company when you set it up.'

Tom returned to what he had been saying.

'The basic principle of a limited company is to create a business structure which separates it from the people who invest in it. In other words, people can invest money in the company and take all the rewards and risks, that is profits or losses, as if they were partners. The difference from a partnership, however, is that if the business goes into 'receivership', or 'liquidation', the people who have invested in it cannot be sued for any more money than they have already invested. That is, they do not risk their other personal property such as savings or homes. These people are a type of investor that we have already established in our business, the 'shareholder'.

'In the same way that the sole proprietor or shareholder owns the business, the shareholders are the owners of the limited company.'

Concepts

SOLE TRADER

This is a common form of business involving just one person. It is a very simple form of business structure, but can involve risks for the person as he or she can personally be held legally responsible for any actions of the business.

PARTNERSHIP

This type of business is defined by the Partnership Act of 1890 and exists 'between persons carrying on business in common with a view to profit'. It is the most common form of business constitution for professions such as doctors, solicitors and accountants. A partnership consists of between 2 and 20 people, but this figure may be exceeded for professions. In most circumstances the liability of the partnership is unlimited, but there are exceptions to this where steps can be taken to limit liability under the Limited Partnerships Act 1907 and 2000.

LIMITED COMPANY

A Limited Company is a common form of business in which the business is a separate legal entity from its owners, the shareholders. There are two main types of company, 'Private Limited Company' and 'Public Limited Company'.

The Companies Act, 1985, specifies that a company

cannot be registered as a Public Limited Company unless it has a minimum allotted share capital of £50,000, at least one quarter of which has actually been paid. It must also have at least two shareholders and two directors. Public companies can have their shares listed on the Stock Exchange, but they have to comply with strict regulations. This type of structure is common in large businesses seeking access to large amounts of capital.

The Companies Act, 1985, defines a Private Limited Company as 'any company that is not a public company'. Private limited companies have no authorised minimum share capital. A private company is only required to have one director and, since 1992, it can be formed with only one member. This type of structure is common in small businesses.

RECEIVERSHIP, LIQUIDATION

A business becomes 'insolvent' when its debts exceed its assets or ability to pay those debts. The treatment of insolvent companies is covered by the Insolvency Act 1986 and subsequent amendments.

The first stage is often to enter a voluntary arrangement between the company and the people to whom it owes money to agree a scheme of reduced or delayed debt payments. If this fails or is not acceptable, the company may be put into 'administration' whereby the bankruptcy court appoints an Administrator who takes over the running of the company.

If the Administrator is successful in running the company it will pay off its debts and be returned to the control of its previous management. If unsuccessful, however, the company is put into 'receivership' whereby the Administrator may continue to run the company while selling assets to pay off specific debts such as debentures secured by fixed charges.

If matters get worse, the Administrator will wind up or

'liquidate' the company. In this situation the business will not recover and all assets are sold off to clear debts as far as possible. There is a clearly defined order for paying off different types of debt in these circumstances, with the Inland Revenue and employees at the head of the queue and shareholders last in the queue.

18

Who Runs the Business?

'Although the shareholders own the limited company, they do not necessarily run the business on a day to day basis. As you will be aware, large companies have thousands of shareholders and it would be impossible for all of those people to run the business, even if they wanted to.

'By the way, does anyone here own shares?'

Several people held up their hands.

'You see what I mean,' continued Tom, 'you are not involved in the day to day running of those companies whose shares you own. What you can do, as shareholders, even if you don't realise it, is to attend the 'Annual General Meeting' of those companies and vote for the 'Board Of Directors'.

'It is the directors who run the business on a day to day basis. In turn they will appoint managers, but they are ultimately answerable to you, the shareholders, who own the business.'

At this point Tom decided that it was time to return to the theme of the coffee business and to explain how all of this fitted together.

'Tony, Mike and Rajiv, you will now have realised that you are the shareholders in our coffee business. You are the people who will actually own the business and keep any profits that are made. Equally, if it all goes disastrously wrong, you will each lose your £20 Share.'

The three shareholders nodded, showing that they realised what they were undertaking.

'As shareholders it is up to you to appoint directors. I suggest that you appoint at least two.'

Rajiv indicated that he would be happy to act as both a director and shareholder, but the other two were less interested.

'Gill, you were the one who first complained about the coffee. How about being a director and making sure that everything is done properly?' asked Rajiv.

Gill blushed and replied, 'I think that I have got no option but to accept. Yes, I'll be a director.'

Tom sat down at his desk and then spoke. 'Thank you, everyone. We now know who will own the coffee business as shareholders, we know who will run it as directors, so all that we need now is to draw up some rules to govern how it is run. I propose that we have two sets of rules.

'Firstly, we need rules to establish the basic administration of the business. In a limited company these are known as the 'Articles Of Association'.

'Secondly, we need a set of rules to give to the college and other people who may deal with the business who want to know what it is all about. In a limited company these rules are known as the 'Memorandum Of Association'.'

Tom noticed that it was time to close the lesson, but added one more comment.

'By the way, everyone. You realise that we are establishing our coffee business along the lines of a limited company. Please note that whilst we shall run it as if it were a limited company, I do not propose that we go through the formal process of actually forming a limited company. That is to say, we shall not go to the expense and trouble of 'Company Incorporation' at 'Companies House'.

'Instead, we shall behave in all ways like a limited company as our purpose here is simply to provide an example of how businesses and companies work.'

Concepts

ANNUAL GENERAL MEETING

The Annual General Meeting ('AGM') is the meeting that a company is required to hold every year and which the shareholders can attend to consider various aspects of the running of the company. Although a wide range of topics can be discussed and voted upon at the AGM, Company Law requires certain topics to be addressed which include the election of directors, review of the annual report and accounts, payments of dividends to shareholders, and appointment of auditors.

DIRECTORS, BOARD OF DIRECTORS

A director is an official of the company appointed annually at the AGM by the shareholders to run the company on their behalf. Although a director may also be a shareholder, he or she does not have ownership simply by being a director. In larger companies directors will often be appointed to specific functions, such as Production Director, Sales Director, or Finance Director. The directors operate collectively as the 'Board Of Directors' and normally appoint one of their members to have overall responsibility as 'Managing Director'.

Salaried directors with day-to-day responsibilities are normally described as 'executive directors'. External advisors to the company, such as bankers or industry experts, are sometimes appointed to the Board as 'non-executive directors' to provide expertise at periodic meetings in return for fees.

ARTICLES OF ASSOCIATION

The Articles Of Association of the company are its internal rules and regulations. The contents of the articles are decided by the shareholders, but in practice are usually based on standard drafts in the Companies Acts. The Articles fix the manner in which the directors and shareholders of the company are to act, both amongst themselves and in relation to each other. They will contain, for example, the powers of directors, the conduct of meetings, the dividend and voting rights assigned to various classes of shareholders, and other miscellaneous rules and regulations.

MEMORANDUM OF ASSOCIATION

The Memorandum of Association is a legal document that is required by Company Law to govern the relationship between the company and third parties. It must contain certain key details including the name of the company, its objects, the country in which it is situated, and details of its share capital.

COMPANY INCORPORATION

Company Incorporation is the process by which a company is legally formed. It involves drawing up a Memorandum of Association, preparation of Articles of Association, obtaining a Certificate of Incorporation from Companies House, issuing share capital and appointing directors.

The Companies Acts that lay down the law relating to companies provide guidance in many of these matters. In practice, anyone wishing to form a new company will often buy an 'off the shelf' company which has been incorporated by a firm specialising in the complexities of company formation. The new owner will then take the necessary steps to change the name of the company and to appoint new directors and shareholders. Using this process a company can be set up in a matter of hours if required.

COMPANIES HOUSE

Companies House is the office of the 'Registrar of Companies' who maintains records of all limited companies in the UK. All companies must lodge copies of their Articles and Memorandum of Association at Companies House, together with an 'Annual Return' detailing key information about the directors and shareholders. Larger companies must also file copies of their annual report and accounts.

Any member of the public can inspect these records for a small fee to gain background information on a particular company. This public accountability is in recognition of the fact that limited liability increases the risk for anyone dealing with the company, and is particularly useful for any potential lender to the company.

19

Introducing Book-keeping

'Time to stop talking about it, let's get on with it!' said Tom at the start of the next lesson. 'We've done the planning for the business, the market research, the financial planning, and deciding on the business constitution. Now let's put our money on the table and get started!'

As agreed, the three shareholders produced £20 each, Dave the debenture holder £30, and Tom as banker £10.

'The first thing to do,' said Tom, 'is to make a note of the money received and where it has come from. This is your introduction to the subject of book-keeping.'

Knowing from many years' experience that this subject would not immediately interest many people, Tom raised his voice.

'For those of you who are thinking of setting up a business, or who currently run a business, this is an important subject as it is a key aspect of the day-to-day operations that will almost certainly involve you at some point.

'Those of you who work in large organisations should also pay attention as you will get an insight into the routine tasks of the finance departments where you work. You will also appreciate how the bills and invoices that are sent to you for your approval to pay are handled and processed by the finance department, and how they are subsequently reported back to you in the accounts that you receive as budget holders and cost centre managers.'

Having made sure that everyone was now listening, Tom continued.

'Please note that there are two aspects to this. First of all, we need to record the amount of money received.'

Tom produced an exercise book and opened it at the first blank double page. Across the top of the page he wrote 'Cash Account'. On the left hand page he wrote 'Debenture – Dave £30'.

'That's recorded that we have received £30 for the debenture.'

He then turned several pages in the book and headed up another blank double page with 'Debentures Account'. On the right hand page he wrote 'Cash – Dave £30'.

'And that is the second entry, which has recorded where the money has come from.'

He held the exercise book up for everyone to see:

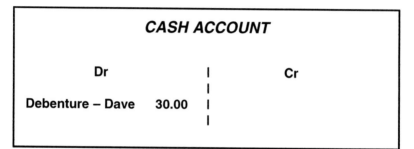

'This is a basic but very important feature of accounting. As you have just seen here, there are two aspects to any transaction: what you get and what you give in return. In the case of the debenture we receive the cash (which is an 'asset' in accounting terms), and in return we give the debenture (a promise to repay), a 'liability' in accounting terms. In the case of a purchase, we receive the goods (assets) and we pay the supplier, either in cash (a corresponding *reduction* in assets) or in the form of a promise to pay in the future (a liability). And so on.

'As we saw above, assets we receive are entered on the left-hand side – known as the 'debit' column – and the corresponding liabilities or reductions in assets are entered in a right-hand column – the 'credit' column. In this way the totals in your left-hand columns will always exactly match the totals in your right-hand columns.'

He then repeated the exercise for the £60 share capital and the £10 bank loan, entering both amounts in the Cash Account (in the left-hand column), and opening new double-pages headed 'Share Capital Account' and 'Bank Loan Account' to record where the money had come from (in the right-hand column).

'Each of these double pages is called an 'Account', and this exercise book is now what we call a 'ledger'. By long-standing tradition, as I mentioned earlier, when we record something on the left-hand side of the account we call it a 'debit', whilst an entry on the right-hand side is called a 'credit'.

'You have probably heard of debits and credits before, and they are at the heart of keeping basic financial records, which is otherwise known as 'Book-keeping'. By recognising that every transaction has two aspects to it, we make two accounting entries for each transaction in a process known as 'Double Entry Book-keeping'.

'Although the principle of entering an asset in the left-hand column (the debit column') and a liability in the right-hand column (the 'credit column') is apparently straightforward, it can sometimes be confusing to know when to make a debit entry and when to make a credit entry. If in doubt, just remember this simple rule that will help you deal with the majority of situations.'

Tom wrote the following sentences on the board:

Any cash received into the business is recorded in the cash account as a debit. A corresponding credit is made in the account of the person, company or item that paid the cash.

Any cash paid out of the business is recorded in the cash account as a credit. A corresponding debit is made in the account of the person, company or item that is being paid the cash.

At that moment Tony spoke up. 'You talk about a cash account, but would it be any different if the money was held in a bank account?'

'None at all,' replied Tom, guessing what Tony's next question would be.

'Well,' said Tony, 'if we paid our total of £100 into the bank, which would be recorded as a debit entry, the bank would give us a statement saying that we have a *credit* balance of £100! How do you explain that?'

'You are absolutely right,' responded Tom, 'and you have hit on one of the first problems to students of book-keeping. But what you must realise is this.

'When the bank sends you a statement, it is showing you a copy of the bank's financial records, not yours. For them your account represents a liability – money that they owe you. When they receive £100 they debit the bank's own cash account and credit *your* account as their customer.

'It's all the same thing, just looking at it from their point of view, not yours.'

The expression on Tony's face showed that he was slowly grasping the point and understanding it.

Tom picked up the ledger and walked over to the board.

'As you will appreciate, all of the debits and credits we have recorded will total to equal amounts. If they don't we have made a mistake somewhere. Let's make a list of them, which is what is known as a 'Trial Balance'.'

Tom wrote down the following :

```
┌─────────────────────────────────────────────────┐
│                 TRIAL BALANCE                     │
│                                                   │
│                          Dr          Cr           │
│                                                   │
│   Bank                 100.00                      │
│                                                   │
│   Debentures                        30.00          │
│                                                   │
│   Shareholders                      60.00          │
│                                                   │
│   Bank loan                         10.00          │
│                        ─────────────────          │
│                        100.00      100.00          │
└─────────────────────────────────────────────────┘
```

'As you see, all of the debits and all of the credits total to the same amount, so I don't think that we have made any mistakes with our book-keeping. Now, let's get on with spending the money and starting the business.'

Tom then passed £80 to Gill who was given the task of buying the two coffee machines, and £20 to Kim who volunteered to buy the first batch of ingredients.

Concepts

ACCOUNT

An account is a structured record of monetary transactions, held within an accounting system, relating to a customer, supplier, income, expenditure, asset or liability. It can be recorded on a single sheet of paper in a traditional hand-written (or 'manual') accounting system, or recorded and displayed as a detailed screen of information in a computerised accounting system.

DEBIT

A debit is an entry to an account which records a certain type of transaction. By convention, it is recorded on the left-hand side of the account and records one of the following types of transaction:

- receipt or recognition of an asset
- extinguishing a liability
- withdrawal of capital or profits by owners
- recording an expense or a loss

CREDIT

A credit is an entry to an account which records a certain type of transaction. By convention, it is recorded on the right-hand side of the account and records one of the following types of transaction:

- disposal of an asset

- reduction in value of an asset
- incurring or recognition of a liability
- introduction of capital by owners
- receipt of income
- reduction of an expense

BOOK-KEEPING

Book-keeping is the term given to recording the monetary transactions of the business. Traditionally recorded by hand in books of account, the term still applies to modern computer accounting systems where the transactions are entered via a keyboard or other electronic means.

DOUBLE ENTRY BOOK-KEEPING

Double Entry Book-keeping is the most widely used method of book-keeping that recognises that every financial transaction involves the simultaneous receiving and giving of value. Consequently, every financial transaction will involve a debit and a corresponding credit to be recorded in the appropriate accounts within the accounting system.

LEDGER

A ledger is a collection of accounts grouped into a particular category.

TRIAL BALANCE

The Trial Balance is a list of all of the debits and credits in the accounts in a Double Entry Book-keeping system. It follows that if all entries have been made correctly the total debit balances will equal the total credit balances. In traditional hand-written books of account, it was common for mistakes to be made and often the Trial Balance would not be in balance until the errors were identified and corrected. In modern computer accounting systems it is very rare that the Trial Balance does not balance as checks within the programs prevent errors in data entry and additions.

20

The Balance Sheet

At the start of the next lesson Gill triumphantly placed the two new coffee machines on Tom's desk, followed by Kim who unloaded a bag full of coffee and other ingredients. This led to a round of applause from the other members of the class.

'Before we celebrate with our first brew,' said Tom, 'let's just see how we should update our ledger.'

'One moment – I only spent £17.90 on the coffee and ingredients as we have bought less sugar than originally planned. Here's £2.10 change from the £20 you gave me,' said Kim.

Tom opened the ledger and opened a new account called 'Fixed Assets'. He then made a debit entry into this account of 'Coffee Machines £80' with a corresponding £80 credit entry to the bank account.

He then repeated this for all of the amounts spent on purchasing the coffee, milk, sugar and filters. Returning to the page in the ledger that recorded the Cash Account, he calculated the net amount of debits and credits in the account:

CASH ACCOUNT

Dr		Cr	
Total receipts	100.00	Total expenditure	97.90
Balance	2.10		

He then wrote out the revised Trial Balance:

TRIAL BALANCE

	Dr	Cr
Cash Account	2.10	
Debentures		30.00
Shareholders		60.00
Bank loan		10.00
Fixed Assets	80.00	
Coffee	7.50	
Milk	3.60	
Sugar	0.80	
Filters	6.00	
	100.00	100.00

He also made a note that all of the ingredients were unused and held as stock.

'Does everybody understand how we have got to this stage?'

Heads nodded in agreement.

'That's good, and you appreciate that this represents the financial state of the business right now.'

Again, heads nodded.

'But I also think that you will agree that whilst all of these debits and credits are a good way of recording the financial affairs, they do not make what we might call 'user friendly' reading.

'Certainly they mean something to someone who knows about book-keeping, but they are not too helpful to the average person in business.

'To make them more user-friendly I am going to re-arrange them into what is known as the 'Balance Sheet'.'

Tom wrote the following on the board:

COFFEE BUSINESS

Balance Sheet at start of business

	£	£	£
FIXED ASSETS:			
Coffee machines			80.00
CURRENT ASSETS:			
Stock of ingredients	17.90		
Cash in hand	2.10		
		20.00	
CURRENT LIABILITIES:			
Bank loan		(10.00)	
NET CURRENT ASSETS			10.00
(CURRENT ASSETS less CURRENT LIABILITIES)			
TOTAL NET ASSETS			90.00
FINANCED BY:			
Share capital		60.00	
Debenture		30.00	
			£90.00

Tom allowed the class some time to study the Balance Sheet before speaking.

'Don't worry too much about how we have got from the Trial Balance to the Balance Sheet. It's all really just a matter of re-arranging the figures under specific headings.

'And before we go off to enjoy our first cup of coffee, I will let you into a few secrets about accounting.

'First of all, this 'Double Entry Book-keeping' system of debits and credits is nothing new. In fact it was first recorded as being used in commerce in Venice in 1494 by a Franciscan friar called Luca Pacioli who was a friend of Leonardo da Vinci.

'But don't go away with the idea that we are looking at an antiquated system. You see, all computerised accounting systems use these methods. No matter how large, fast or clever the computer, the basic principles and terminology of debit and credit are at the heart of the system.

'And our little exercise book or ledger, containing all of those debits and credits, is known as a 'General Ledger' – it is the master ledger containing records of both sides of every single transaction you make.'

Concepts

BALANCE SHEET

The Balance Sheet is a statement of the financial position of a business at a particular point in time, normally prepared at the end of the financial year. It lists the assets which the firm owns and the corresponding obligations or claims of those groups of people who provided funds to pay for the assets. Most modern Balance Sheets are presented in a fairly standard layout starting with the fixed assets owned by the business. Below this are shown the current assets and current liabilities. The net balance of these items is the 'Net Worth' of the business.

GENERAL LEDGER (Or Nominal Ledger)

The General Ledger is the main ledger of accounts in an accounting system. Although various other ledgers may exist in the accounting system, they are all ultimately linked to the General Ledger and it is from the General Ledger that the Trial Balance is taken. The General Ledger is also sometimes called the Nominal Ledger, but this is now considered to be a rather old-fashioned term.

NET CURRENT ASSETS

Net Current Assets is difference between the current assets and the current liabilities in the Balance Sheet. It is also sometimes referred to as 'working capital'.

NET ASSETS

Net assets is the total of the fixed assets and the net current assets in the Balance Sheet. It is effectively the book value of the business and by definition is equivalent to the Net Worth of the business.

21

Sales Ledger and Purchase Ledger

The first brewing of coffee in the new coffee machines was undertaken in an air of excitement. Everyone recognised the improvement in the quality of the coffee compared with the old machine coffee. There was no doubt that the new business would attract regular business from satisfied customers.

As the year progressed, the business prospered. A large number of cups of coffee were sold each day and the stocks of ingredients were frequently replenished.

After a while, some of the customers of the business asked if they could pay at the end of each month rather than having to bring in the right amount of cash each day. Gill agreed to let them do this, but realised that she would have to keep a careful record of who owed money to the business. She bought another exercise book in which she wrote down details of all of the sales, showing separate details of sales for cash and sales to people who asked for credit.

'Why have you started another exercise book?' Tom asked her. 'I didn't tell you to do that.'

'No,' replied Gill, 'but it just seemed like a good idea to keep track of everything.'

'You are absolutely right,' replied Tom enthusiastically, 'and once again you see that running the business efficiently is largely a question of applying common sense.

'But what are you going to do with that information in your book, which in business jargon is known as a 'Sales Day Book'?'

'I thought that I could summarise it at the end of the month and give you details of the cash taken and a list of who owes us money. I assume that you will want to copy it all into the General Ledger.'

'Yes, that is right, but whilst I can record the total of the cash quite easily, how am I going to open up accounts in our little exercise book for all of those people who owe us money?'

'Simple. Let's get another exercise book and open up accounts for all the people who buy coffee on credit. Whenever they buy coffee, or pay up what they owe, I'll record that information in the second exercise book.'

'Excellent, Gill. Yet again, a common-sense solution to the problem. What you have described is known as a 'Sales Ledger', recording all the people who owe money to the business, otherwise known as 'Debtors'. For that reason the Sales Ledger is also sometimes referred to as the 'Debtors' Ledger'.

'All we need to do is to add in whatever amount you have in the Sales Ledger to what I have in the General Ledger when we produce the Trial Balance. Rather than doing that as an afterthought, we will open another account in the General Ledger which we shall call the 'Sales Ledger Control'. We shall record in this the net amounts showing in your Sales Ledger.'

After a further period of time, the local supermarket which sold the ingredients to the coffee business agreed to open an account and sell on credit. The agreement was that the account should be paid up at the end of each month.

Kim was responsible for buying the ingredients and she copied Gill's method of recording what she had bought. In due course, she found it cheaper to buy the ingredients at several different shops. When she was offered credit terms from more than one shop, this method helped her to keep track of what she had spent and what the business owed to each shop.

The daily record of expenditure was recorded in the 'Purchases Day Book', whilst the details of amounts owed to suppliers who allowed credit terms, known as 'Creditors', were recorded in individual accounts in an exercise book marked 'Purchase Ledger'. Tom opened up a 'Purchase Ledger Control' in his General Ledger to record the overall amount owed to creditors at the end of each month.

Having done this, Tom addressed the class.

'Please would you all note that Gill is now responsible for the Sales Ledger and controls all money coming into the business from sales. Kim, on the other hand, is responsible for the Purchase Ledger and controls money spent by the business.'

Tom noticed a flash of inspiration on Rajiv's face.

'That explains something!' exclaimed Rajiv. 'Whenever I have a query with the invoices for the stationery that my department buys, I contact the finance department of our supplier company to query the charges. Their switchboard telephonist always asks me if I want their Sales Ledger or Purchase Ledger department. I've never really understood what she meant until now!'

'So which department will you ask for from now on?' asked Tom.

'Easy,' replied Rajiv. 'They sell to me so I want their Sales Ledger department.'

'Correct,' replied Tom, and added with a chuckle, 'and now you will appreciate that this stuff about book-keeping can be relevant to you even if you have never set foot inside a finance department!'

Concepts

SALES DAY BOOK

The Sales Day Book is a book used to record invoices issued to customers in order of date and invoice number. This information is subsequently entered into the individual account of each person who has an account with the business, or alternatively recorded as a cash transaction for customers who do not hold accounts with the business.

SALES LEDGER

The Sales Ledger is the ledger that holds the accounts of all customers who are allowed to buy goods or services on credit as opposed to paying cash for each transaction.

DEBTORS, DEBTORS' LEDGER

Debtors are people or organisations that owe money to the business. The major category of debtors is normally the customers recorded in the Sales Ledger. Until a customer pays or 'clears' his account, there is a debit balance showing how much is owed. A debtor is in effect a 'debitor'. For this reason the Sales Ledger is sometimes referred to as the 'Debtors' Ledger'.

PURCHASES DAY BOOK

The Purchases Day Book is a book used to record invoices received from suppliers in date order. This information is subsequently entered into the individual account of each supplier in the Purchase Ledger.

PURCHASE LEDGER

The Purchase Ledger is the ledger that holds the accounts of all suppliers who sell to the business on credit as opposed to paying cash for each transaction.

CREDITORS

Creditors are people or organisations that are owed money by the business. The major category of trade creditors is normally the suppliers recorded in the Purchase Ledger. Until the supplier is paid there is a credit balance showing how much the business owes. (Unlike the debtors' ledger, it is rare to hear the Purchase Ledger referred to as the Creditors' Ledger).

22

Preparing the Accounts

And so the year passed with the coffee business operating to everyone's satisfaction. At the end of the year, Tom decided that it was time to see exactly how the business had performed in financial terms.

'You will recall,' he said, 'that when we set up the business a year ago we prepared two financial documents.

'The first was the budgeted, or forecast, Profit and Loss Account which showed that we expected the business to make a small profit.

'The second was the Balance Sheet at the start of the business. This showed the state of the business at that point in time.

'Just to recap and remind you why we produced both documents I would like to draw a comparison with buying a motor car.

'The forecast Profit and Loss Account is concerned with how well the car is expected to perform and what the likely running costs will be.

'The Balance Sheet is like a manufacturer's specification for a new car, or in the case of a second-hand car it is rather like the MOT certificate. It shows you the state of the car at a particular time.

'If you had bought a car a year ago it is probable that you would want, or even need, to see how well it had performed during the year. Had it gone better or worse than expected? The service history would show you this. In the case of a business, you need to draw up a Profit and Loss Account for the period.

'Similarly, you would want to know the current condition of the car. An inspection or MOT would give you an idea of which parts are working satisfactorily and which need mechanical attention. In business it is the Balance Sheet prepared at the end of the period that gives you some idea of the state of the business.'

Tom knew that the comparison with the motor car was often helpful to students who were not completely clear as to why it was necessary to produce both a Profit and Loss Account and a Balance Sheet.

'We saw that you drew up the Balance Sheet from the Trial Balance, but where does the Profit and Loss Account come from?' asked an alert student in the front row.

'Good question, and the answer is that both of them come from the Trial Balance. Let's take a look at our General Ledger after our first year of trading.'

Tom then copied all of the balances from the General Ledger as a Trial Balance on the board. He then added a third column which he called 'Category'.

In the Category column he marked a 'B' for accounts that would go to the Balance Sheet and a 'P' for accounts that would go to the Profit and Loss Account. Some accounts were marked with both letters indicating that they would be split between the Balance Sheet and the Profit and Loss Account:

TRIAL BALANCE

	Dr	Cr	Category
Bank	55.00		B
Debentures		30.00	B
Shareholders		60.00	B
Bank loan		10.00	B
Fixed Assets	80.00		B
Coffee	290.00		P (used) / B (in stock)
Milk	144.00		P (used) / B (in stock)
Sugar	88.00		P (used) / B (in stock)
Filters	206.00		P (used) / B (in stock)
Electricity	30.00		P (used) / B (owing)
Caretaker's wages	200.00		P
Sales Ledger Control	38.00		B
Purchase Ledger Control		14.00	B
Sales		1,017.00	P
	1,131.00	1,131.00	

'What we now do is to make various adjustments to these accounts, and then we put some of them in the Balance Sheet and the others in the Profit and Loss Account.

'I think that we have said enough about basic book-keeping and I don't want to bore you with too much of the nitty-gritty of accounting techniques.

'At this stage I just want you to be aware that we have to adjust our ingredients to recognise that we still have items in stock that should go into the Balance Sheet as assets of the business. The ingredients shown in the Profit and Loss Account are only what has actually been used up. Similarly, we must make adjustments for items like the electricity which we have used but not yet paid for.

'Kim, please could you tell us the amount and value of our stocks at the year end.'

Kim stood up and read out the following:

'Coffee, 2 boxes, cost £5.00.

'Filters, 3 boxes, cost £6.00.

'Milk, 5 pints, cost £1.80.

'Sugar, 2 bags, cost £1.60.

'That totals to £14.40.'

As Tom made a note of these amounts on the board, Gill the nursing manager raised her hand.

'Is this why I have to fill in a stock level report for my ward at the hospital at the end of each month?' she asked. 'I've never really understood why the hospital finance department ask me to do this.'

'Exactly right,' replied Tom. 'It's all part of the process of making sure that the expenditure on your ward is measured and reported accurately. As the person who is responsible for controlling the expenditure on the ward, it is in your best interest to make sure that these stock sheets are filled in accurately.'

Turning back to face the board again, Tom then produced the following Profit and Loss Account:

COFFEE BUSINESS

Profit and Loss Account
for the 12 months to 200_

	£	£	£
TURNOVER			**1,017.00**
COST OF GOODS SOLD			
Coffee	290.00		
Filters	206.00		
Milk	144.00		
Sugar	88.00		
		728.00	
Less: Closing Stocks			
Coffee	(5.00)		
Filters	(6.00)		
Milk	(1.80)		
Sugar	(1.60)		
		(14.40)	
			713.60
GROSS PROFIT			**303.40**
OVERHEAD COSTS			
Electricity		40.00	
Wages		200.00	
			240.00
NET PROFIT BEFORE INTEREST			
& DEPRECIATION			**63.40**

'At this stage I have called the bottom line 'Net Profit before Interest & Depreciation' because we haven't yet deducted interest payable on Dave's debenture and my loan to the business. Also, we haven't taken off the depreciation we talked about when we prepared our budgeted Profit and Loss Account.

'I recall that when we drew up the paperwork for the debenture and my loan as banker that we should pay 8% rate of interest on the debentures and 10% on my loan.

'Let me see, that works out at interest payable to Dave on the debentures of £2.40, and interest due on my loan of £1.00.

'Also, I remember that the depreciation was to be £20.'

Tom then adjusted the Profit and Loss Account to read as follows:

COFFEE BUSINESS

Profit and Loss Account
for the 12 months to 200_

	£	£	£
TURNOVER			1,017.00
COST OF GOODS SOLD			
Coffee	290.00		
Filters	206.00		
Milk	144.00		
Sugar	88.00		
		728.00	
Less: Closing Stocks			
Coffee	(5.00)		
Filters	(6.00)		
Milk	(1.80)		
Sugar	(1.60)		
		(14.40)	
			713.60
GROSS PROFIT			303.40
OVERHEAD COSTS			
Electricity		40.00	
Wages		200.00	
			240.00
NET PROFIT BEFORE INTEREST & DEPRECIATION			63.40
Interest payable		3.40	
Depreciation		20.00	
			23.40
NET PROFIT			40.00

Tom also drew up the following Balance Sheet:

COFFEE BUSINESS

Balance Sheet at ....

	£	£	£
FIXED ASSETS:			
Coffee machines		80.00	
Less: Depreciation		20.00	
			60.00
CURRENT ASSETS:			
Stock of ingredients	14.40		
Debtors	38.00		
Cash in hand	55.00		
		107.40	
CURRENT LIABILITIES:			
Creditors	(14.00)		
Electricity owing	(10.00)		
Interest payable	(3.40)		
Bank loan	(10.00)		
		(37.40)	
NET CURRENT ASSETS			70.00
TOTAL NET ASSETS			130.00
FINANCED BY:			
Share capital		60.00	
Profit		40.00	
Owner's equity			100.00
Debenture			30.00
			£130.00

Concepts

OWNERS' EQUITY

Owners' Equity is that part of the net worth of the business that is due to the owners of the business. It is normally calculated as the sum of the owners' investment in the business (e.g. shares) plus profit in the business (which is effectively the property of the owners).

23

The Return on Investment

The class spent some time studying the Profit and Loss Account and Balance Sheet before Tom spoke again.

'The adjustments for items like the stock and depreciation would normally be entered, or 'posted', to the General Ledger. I'm not going to bother with the details of that now. What is more important is that you are aware of the general principles of how the debits and credits in the General Ledger end up in the Profit and Loss Account or the Balance Sheet.

'And another thing. Don't get too concerned about the exact layout and content of the Profit and Loss Account and Balance Sheet. For our purposes there are no hard and fast rules, but you should be aware that the 'Published Accounts' of a Limited Company have to comply with various rules laid down under the Companies Acts and special accounting guidelines drafted by the main professional accounting bodies. These are known as 'Accounting Standards'. Similarly, there are various rules that apply to reporting financial results for Public Services. Also, many organisations have to have the accuracy of their accounts checked by an 'auditor'.'

Tom then turned to face the Profit and Loss Account that he had drawn on the board.

'There are a couple more items that we must think about on our Profit and Loss Account.

'First of all, there is the question of profit and the shareholders. This will be of interest to you three shareholders, Tony, Mike and Rajiv.

'We originally estimated that our net profit would be £28, but the good news is that it is better than expected at £40. Now, you as shareholders have to decide what to do with that profit.

'You can either take it out of the business as a cash payment which is known as a 'Dividend', or you can leave it in the business as 'Retained Profit'. Of course, if you wish, you may take part of it as dividend and leave part as retained profit. It is up to you as owners of the business, and what you decide is known as 'Distribution Policy'.'

'Surely it is best to take it all out, isn't it?' asked Mike.

'Yes, you could if you want to, but what if next year things don't go so well? How will you cover the loss? What if you decide that you would like to expand the activities of the business and you need money to invest in more assets?'

Mike thought about this for a moment and nodded thoughtfully.

'I suppose it's best to think about how much the business may need in the future, like you have said, and then take just part of the profit out as a dividend.'

'Exactly right, and that is exactly what many businesses do. But before you do that, what about my bank loan of £10? As you now have £55 cash in hand, how about paying my loan off? There is no point in having surplus cash in hand and then borrowing unnecessarily from the bank and paying interest. If you pay off my loan you will save the £1 interest charge on next year's Profit & Loss Account.'

Tom paused to let this point sink in.

'And there is a second point that we must consider. Our coffee business is, fortunately, our own informal business. Strictly speaking, however, it is like all businesses and is therefore potentially subject to pay tax on its profits. This is a very complicated area, and at this stage I simply want you to be aware that our Net Profit should strictly be stated as 'Net Profit before Taxation'.'

The mention of tax brought a groan of disapproval from the class.

'Cheer up,' responded Tom. 'No-one wants to pay tax, but at least if you have to pay tax it means that you have made a profit.

'Let's think about that profit for a moment.

'You three shareholders each bought a £20 share in the business. After one year of trading you are each entitled to one third of the Net

Profit of £40 which works out at £13.33 each.

'On an investment of £20, a profit or 'Earnings Per Share' of £13.33 is equivalent to a 'Return On Capital Employed' of 67%.

'I think you will agree that 67% is a very attractive return on your investment and much better than any bank or building society could offer. On the other hand, though, you could have lost the lot. That's what being a shareholder and taking risks is all about.'

Concepts

PUBLISHED ACCOUNTS

All Public Limited Companies (PLCs) and Private Limited Companies above a specified size have to publish their accounts and file copies at Companies House. Various rules prescribe the contents of the published accounts based on the requirements of the Companies Acts and requirements of various professional accounting bodies.

COMPANIES ACTS

Much of the law relating to companies in the UK is laid down in a series of Companies Acts, the major provisions being in the Companies Acts of 1948, 1967, 1976, 1981, 1985 and 1989.

ACCOUNTING STANDARDS

Accounting standards are authoritative statements of how particular types of transaction and other events should be reflected in financial statements. Accounting standards issued by the Accounting Standards Board are designated 'Financial Accounting Standards' (or FASs). Those issued by its predecessor bodies, and adopted by the Board when it was created in 1990, are designated 'Statements of Standard Accounting Practice' (or SSAPs).

Companies legislation does not directly require compliance with accounting standards. However, the Companies Act, 1985, requires accounts (other than those prepared by small or medium-sized companies) to state whether they have been prepared in accordance with applicable accounting standards and to give particulars of any material departure from those standards and the reasons for it.

AUDIT

All limited companies above a specified size are required to have their accounting records, Balance Sheet and Profit & Loss Accounts examined by a suitably qualified auditor to ensure that they show a 'true and fair view' of the company's finances. A note to this effect signed by the auditor will then be included in the company's published accounts. The 'true and fair view' is intended to protect the interests of shareholders and all other parties who have an involvement or interest in the company.

DIVIDEND, DISTRIBUTION POLICY, RETAINED PROFIT

A dividend is a distribution of the profits of a limited company paid to a shareholder, usually in the form of cash. Part of the financial management of a company involves 'Distribution Policy' which determines the proportion of profit to be distributed to shareholders as dividends and how much profit should be held back within the company ('Retained Profit') to help finance future growth or cover potential losses.

TAXATION

The taxation rules that apply to businesses are extremely complicated, but in simple terms the net profits of sole traders and partnerships are subject to 'Income Tax' whilst companies pay 'Corporation Tax'.

EARNINGS PER SHARE (EPS)

Earnings per share (EPS) is calculated as the net profit

after tax due to shareholders divided by the number of shares. It is not the same as dividend per share as it takes into account the amount of retained profit attributable to each share.

RETURN ON CAPITAL EMPLOYED (ROCE)

Return On Capital Employed (ROCE) is calculated as the net profit before tax divided by the capital employed. It is expressed as a percentage, and provides a measure of the profitability of the business.

24

Where Has the Cash Gone?

'There is one thing that is puzzling me,' said Tony. 'I understand how we have arrived at our Net Profit figure of £40, but I don't really understand why the bank account is now standing at £55. Shouldn't the two totals be the same?'

'That's a question that many students ask,' replied Tom, 'but you are forgetting our definition of profit. We said at a very early stage that profit is an increase in wealth and, as you know, wealth can be held in many forms. A wealthy person may have a large house and an expensive car but may not have much cash at the bank. It is exactly the same for a business, where the wealth of the business can be held in many ways such as fixed assets, stocks and so on.

'I understand your concern though, and for that reason I am going to draw up a 'Source And Application Of Funds Statement'.

'I don't want you to worry too much about the exact details of how we do this. All that I want you to know is that this statement, also known as a 'Funds Flow Statement', is intended to explain what has happened to the cash in the business during the year.'

Tom began to write on the board.

'Look carefully at each line. There are no words or definitions that are new to you. You should be able to follow what is going on.'

COFFEE BUSINESS

Source and Application of Funds
for the 12 months ended.........

SOURCES:

	£	£	£
CAPITAL INTRODUCED			
Shares issued		60.00	
Debentures issued		30.00	
Bank Loan		10.00	
			100.00
CASH FLOW FROM OPERATIONS			
Net profit		40.00	
Add back depreciation		20.00	
			60.00
NET CASH INFLOW			160.00

APPLICATIONS:

	£	£
PURCHASE OF FIXED ASSETS		80.00
INCREASE IN WORKING CAPITAL		
Increase in stock of ingredients	14.40	
Increase in debtors	38.00	
less:		
Increase in creditors (*excluding bank loan**)	(27.40)	
		25.00
CASH IN HAND		55.00
		160.00

(*including the interest owed, but not the amount borrowed, which is already featured in Capital Introduced at the top of the page.)

'As I have said before, don't get too worried about the exact layout of this Funds Flow Statement. Just remember that all we are trying to do is explain how money, or cash, has come into the business and where it went out.'

'How does this tie up with our original Cash Flow Forecast?' asked Tony.

'It's really all one and the same thing. The difference is that the Forecast looked at what was expected to happen to the cash on a quarterly basis, whilst the Funds Flow Statement summarises what has actually happened to the cash by the end of the year.

In both cases, you will note that we had to take out the depreciation charge and put in what we had actually spent in cash on the Fixed Assets. You will remember that we talked about that when we did the Cash Flow Forecast.'

Tom looked at the class. There were a few frowns and puzzled expressions as people studied the Funds Flow Statement, but then again, he thought to himself, there always are. He knew from experience that it was best to leave people to study this quietly and think about what he had said. Some people would grasp it quickly, others would take a little longer.

Concepts

SOURCE & APPLICATION OF FUNDS, FUNDS FLOW STATEMENT

The Source & Application of Funds Statement is a report that shows how cash has been generated from the normal trading activities of the business and any other sources (such as capital invested or assets sold) followed by details of how the cash has been spent or used. It provides a link between the Profit & Loss Account and the Balance Sheet and is useful in providing a link between profit and cash balances.

25

Management Accounts

'There is something else we should do at this point. We know that our business has done slightly better than we originally expected, but what exactly has happened, where and why?

'Does anyone have any suggestions?'

The answer to this was immediately obvious to Rajiv, the computer salesman, who was used to seeing similar reports in his work.

'I think that this is where we put the budgeted Profit and Loss Account alongside the actual Profit and Loss Account for the year and see how they compare. We identify the differences between them and look for the causes.'

'That's right,' said Tom. 'This sounds familiar to you so perhaps you would like to demonstrate this on the board for all of us.'

Tom handed Rajiv copies of the budgeted Profit and Loss Account and the year end Profit and Loss Account. To make the layout and sums easier, Rajiv deducted the closing stocks of ingredients and changed the 'Cost of Goods Sold' line to 'Cost of Goods Used'. He then added the additional column headed 'Difference' and wrote the following on the board:

COFFEE BUSINESS

Profit and Loss Account
for the 12 months ended.........

	BUDGET	ACTUAL	DIFFERENCE	
	£	£	£	%
TURNOVER	960.00	1,017.00	57.00	5.9
COST OF GOODS USED:				
Coffee	240.00	285.00	(45.00)	(18.8)
Filters	192.00	200.00	(8.00)	(4.2)
Milk	144.00	142.20	1.80	1.2
Sugar	96.00	86.40	9.60	10.0
	672.00	713.60	(41.60)	(6.2)
GROSS PROFIT	288.00	303.40	15.40	5.3
OVERHEAD COSTS				
Electricity	40.00	40.00	0.00	0.0
Caretaker's wages	200.00	200.00	0.00	0.0
	240.00	240.00	0.00	0.0
NET PROFIT BEFORE CAPITAL CHARGES	48.00	63.40	15.40	32.1
Interest Payable	3.40	3.40	0.00	0.0
Depreciation	20.00	20.00	0.00	0.0
	23.40	23.40	0.00	0.0
NET PROFIT	24.60	40.00	15.40	63.4

'Rajiv, that is excellent. Obviously you have seen something like this before. Tell me, though, why have you put brackets round some of the numbers in the way you have?'

'That's easy,' replied Rajiv. 'I used to get very confused about the difference column. Sometimes there would be a bracket, other times there would be a minus sign.

'I asked the chap who works in the accounts department what it all meant. He explained that a bracket or a negative sign meant the same thing, that the number was negative. This still confused me, because it all seemed to get complicated and contradictory if we were talking about costs or income. In the end we agreed just to use the bracket sign and, in our company at least, a bracket could be interpreted as being 'bad news' or 'worse than planned'.'

'That's a very good way of looking at it, and one that is well worth keeping in mind,' said Tom. 'Let's just quickly talk a bit more about this.'

He coughed before continuing.

'The 'Difference' column is often known as a 'Variance', and what we are doing by highlighting and examining those variances is sometimes called 'Variance Analysis'.

'We can see that we sold £57.00 more coffee more than we anticipated, but unfortunately we also spent £41.60 more on ingredients than planned. That is hardly surprising, though, as more cups of coffee sold would obviously require more ingredients. Interestingly, we have not used quite as many ingredients per cup of coffee as we expected, particularly sugar, which is reflected in the better than expected Gross Profit.

'The Overhead Costs and Capital Charges are exactly what we expected and consequently don't show a variance. Putting all of this together explains why the Net Profit is showing a favourable variance of £15.40.'

Tom paused whilst people looked at the numbers and thought about what he had said.

'This is a very important and useful management report. Although you all now know a bit about how accounts and reports are prepared, I don't suppose that any of you have plans to become accountants.'

This produced a mixture of muttered comments and laughter.

'As managers, however, I expect that you will increasingly see reports like this. In many organisations, they are produced each month as part of the 'Management Accounts', and extracts are circulated to the appropriate cost centre managers as budget statements.'

Tom stopped and smiled. 'At least now, I hope, they will make more sense to you!'

Concepts

VARIANCES, VARIANCE ANALYSIS

A variance is the difference between a planned or budgeted result and the subsequent actual result. By analysing variances it is possible to identify problem areas and take the appropriate corrective action. Variance analysis is often applied as part of the budgetary control process.

MANAGEMENT ACCOUNTS

Management accounts are accounts produced for internal use within an organisation to assist management in running the company efficiently and profitably. They provide much greater detail than published accounts, and in most medium-sized and large organisations are produced on a monthly basis. With the widespread use of desk-top computers and low cost accounting software packages, there has been a significant increase in the use of management accounts in business in recent years as the information can be produced 'in-house' relatively quickly and easily.

26

The Year End

With the first year of college over, Tom addressed the class for the last time before the vacation break.

'Before we pack up, I suggest that you might like to spend a short while getting together to discuss how our coffee business has done over the past year. In a limited company, that is what happens when they call the Annual General Meeting. Those of you who are shareholders can take the opportunity to raise matters for discussion and take any necessary decisions. Again, in a limited company this is what the rather complicated business of 'Resolutions' is all about.'

By 5 o'clock, the talking was all over and the class began to break up and file out. During the meeting, Rajiv had mentioned that he would not be able to continue with the class as he had been promoted to a new regional management position and would be moving to the new job.

'What do I do about my shares?' he asked.

Several members of the class immediately offered to buy them from him. Some people were even prepared to offer him more than the £20 value as they were clearly offering a very good return. As the noise died down Tom held up his hand to speak.

'That was a very spontaneous demonstration of how shares can be bought and sold in a business. And what's more, we even saw that the price at which shares can be traded is not necessarily the same as their face value. We shall learn more about that when we cover the workings of the 'Stock Exchange'. But that is not until next term.'

The last person to walk out of the room was Gill, the nurse. As she reached the door Tom called over to her.

'Have a nice break, Gill, and I'll see you next term. Have you got any plans for the vacation?'

'Not really,' replied Gill. 'We are very busy at the hospital at the moment, and besides, I'm in charge of setting up a special new feature on the ward.'

'Oh, yes, what's that?'

'It's a coffee facility for patients and visitors.'

She smiled at Tom, and then they both laughed.

Concepts

RESOLUTIONS

Much of the business that is conducted at the company general meetings is by way of 'resolution' whereby votes are cast by shareholders attending the meeting. Company law specifies various types of resolution ('ordinary, special, extraordinary and elective') for different types of decision about how the company is to be run and conduct its affairs.

STOCK EXCHANGE

The UK Stock Exchange is the market in London that deals in the buying and selling of company shares. Not all company shares are sold on the Stock Exchange, only those of PLC companies that meet the stringent requirements of the Exchange. The main purpose of the Stock Exchange is to provide a means for a company to issue and sell new shares to raise additional capital, and also to provide a means for investors to buy and sell existing shares.

Index